EDITOR: LEE JOHNSON

OSPREY MILITARY | **WARRIOR SERIES** | **2**

WAFFEN-SS SOLDIER
1940–1945

Text by
BRUCE QUARRIE
Colour plates by
JEFFREY BURN

Published in 1993 by
Osprey Publishing Ltd
Michelin House,
81 Fulham Rd, London SW3 6RB
and Aukland, Melbourne, Singapore and Toronto

Reprinted 1993

ISBN 1 85532 288 9

Filmset in Great Britain
Printed through Bookbuilders in Hong Kong

Publisher's Note
Readers may wish to study this title in conjunction
with the following Osprey publications:

MAA 34   *Waffen-SS*
MAA 234   *German Combat
            Equipments 1939–45,*
Elite 11   *Ardennes 1944 Peiper
            & Skorzeny*
Campaign 1 *Normandy 1944*
Campaign 24 *Arnhem 1944.*

For a catalogue of all books published by Osprey Military
please write to:

**The Marketing Manager,
Consumer Catalogue Department,
Osprey Publishing Ltd,
Michelin House, 81 Fulham Road,
London SW3 6RB**

HISTORICAL BACKGROUND

The Waffen-SS was a unique phenomenon in military history, and comparisons with other famous bodies of fighting men—such as the Praetorian Guard of the Caesars which is most commonly cited—fall apart on close examination. The Waffen-SS was one of the end products of an ailing and disillusioned society at odds with itself and the world. That society itself was born of defeat in the Great War and the horrendous effects of the Depression; it was a society which, while paying lip service to democracy, really felt it needed and wanted strong leadership. What it got was Adolf Hitler and the NSDAP—the National Socialist German Workers' Party.

The key words in the Party's name were 'National' and 'German', and from the moment the NSDAP was elected to power and Hitler appointed

Forerunner of the Waffen-SS, the 'Stosstruppe Hitler' formed by one of Hitler's two chauffeur/bodyguards, Julius Schreck (centre, with moustache) in 1923. The basic SA 'uniform' – with wide variations evident – is complemented by black ski caps. These are adorned with a white metal Totenkopf or 'death's head' badge, a symbol Schreck adopted from the Freikorps'

Erhardt Brigade of which he had been a member. This was really nothing new, since the 'skull and crossbones' has an illustrious history in many nations as a light cavalry symbol in particular, and was adopted by the Wehrmacht's Panzer forces as well as the SS; but within the Waffen-SS it acquired specific connotations (see text). (Bildarchiv Preussicher Kulturbesitz, Berlin)

Rather more resplendent than the original 'Stosstruppe', the 120-strong 'Stabwache' assembled on the steps of Munich's Braunehause in 1930. They still wear brown shirts but uniformly with black caps, ties, trousers and boots. Josef 'Sepp' Dietrich is third from left in the front row. (Bildarchiv Preussicher, Berlin)

Chancellor in 1933, the German people were not allowed to forget either. This is the first essential in understanding the motivation of those who would later serve in the ranks of the Waffen-SS (literally, 'Weapon-SS').

It would be pointless, here, to examine the finer points of Nazi ideology, but it is easy to pick the critical elements out of the Party's manifesto. This called for the unification of all Germanic peoples, specifically excluded Jews from any right to German citizenship, demanded a halt to all non-German immigration and expressed the right of the German people to *Lebensraum*—living room: a clear declaration of an aggressive expansionist policy. And the Waffen-SS was to become one of the keenest weapons in the exploitation of that policy.

The actual title 'Waffen-SS' did not become official until 1940, but for convenience will be used throughout to differentiate the armed branch of Heinrich Himmler's empire from the other tentacles of the Schutzstaffel, or 'Protection Squad'. Even the title 'SS' only came into existence after Hitler's release from Landsberg jail in December 1924, following his attempted take-over of the Bavarian state government in the Munich 'beer hall putsch'. Prior to this, the nucleus of what was to become the SS was known as the Stosstruppe (assault troop) Hitler and consisted of a mere twelve men organised under one of Hitler's chauffeurs, Julius Schreck, as a personal bodyguard for the man who would later adopt the title Der Führer—'The Leader'.

From this tiny beginning the Waffen-SS would ultimately grow to a strength of some 910,000 men—an astonishing figure, but still only a tenth of the size of the regular army at its peak. Perhaps a more relevant comparison is that, in 1943–44, the seven premier SS divisions totalled nearly a quarter of the Panzer (armoured) strength available to the Wehrmacht (armed forces), and, on their own, contributed significantly to delaying the defeat of Germany for so long. (It should be pointed out that although the Waffen-SS was subordinated operationally to the orders of the Oberkommando der Wehrmacht, or Armed Forces High Command, it was never an integral part of the Wehrmacht.)

The real growth of the Waffen-SS stemmed from 1929, when Heinrich Himmler—a mild-mannered, fastidious, but ruthlessly ambitious man—was appointed Reichsführer-SS. Over the next ten years he expanded his empire rapidly, especially after Hitler repudiated the Treaty of Versailles which had ended the First World War and reintroduced conscription in 1935. By the time Germany went to war in September 1939 Himmler was able to field three reinforced regiments (the Leibstandarte 'Adolf Hitler', Standarte 'Deutschland' and Standarte 'Germania') with a fourth, Austrian, regiment undergoing training. In addition, there were the members of the Totenkopfverbände (Death's Head Band), originally raised as concentration camp guards, who would by the following year constitute an entire motorised infantry division.

By the end of the war, 38 Waffen-SS divisions (of highly variable quality) would have been raised — some of the later ones divisions in name only. Collectively, they would earn themselves the dubious sobriquet 'soldiers of destruction'.

CHRONOLOGY

1924 Title 'SS' becomes official.
1929 Himmler appointed Reichsführer-SS.
1933 Hitler becomes Chancellor.
1935 Reintroduction of conscription.
1936 Establishment of SS Inspectorate and training schools.
1939 Invasion of Poland; Leibstandarte and SS-V participate with 'Totenkopf' in second line.
1940 Invasion of France, Holland and Belgium. Title 'Waffen-SS' becomes official. Expansion authorised and recruitment of non-German volunteers begins.
1941 Leibstandarte and 'Reich' take part in invasions of Greece and Yugoslavia then, together with 'Totenkopf', the 'Polizei' Division and 'Wiking', the invasion of Russia.
1942 Beginning of transformation of Leibstandarte, 'Das Reich' and 'Totenkopf' into Panzergrenadier divisions; 'Wiking' reaches Rostov but escapes entrapment at Stalingrad.
1943 Creation of I SS Panzer Korps; battle of Kursk; Allies land in Sicily and Italy; Italy surrenders.
1944 D-Day. Leibstandarte, 'Das Reich', 'Hitler Jugend' and 'Götz von Berlichingen' decimated and pulled out to be re-formed; July bomb plot on Hitler's life results in his placing even more reliance on the Waffen-SS; 'Hohenstaufen' and 'Frundsberg' defeat Allied Rhine crossing at Arnhem; creation of Sixth (SS) Panzer Army for the Battle of the Bulge; in Russia, 'Wiking' decimated at Cherkassy; beginning of final Russian summer offensive; Warsaw Uprising suppressed by Waffen-SS; Russians enter Belgrade, occupy Romania and surround Budapest.
1945 Start of last Russian winter offensive; heavy fighting in Hungary; Ardennes offensive defeated; fall of Budapest; Allies cross Rhine and link with Russians on the Elbe; Hitler commits suicide; fall of Berlin; Germany surrenders unconditionally; SS declared a criminal organisation and war crimes tribunals begin.

A troop of the SS-Kavallerie Brigade in 1941. This was subsequently (1942) enlarged into the 8th SS Kavallerie Division 'Florian Geyer' under the command of 'Willi' Bittrich and, later, Hermann Fegelein. (Bundesarchiv, Koblenz)

APPEARANCE

In general terms, and certainly during the early part of the war, the Waffen-SS grenadier wore much the same clothing and carried the same personal equipment as his counterpart in the army. There were minor variations, for example in the exact cut and styling of tunics, sidecaps and field caps; rank insignia was totally different because the Waffen-SS used essentially the same rank structure as the old SA stormtroopers. The national eagle was worn on the left arm instead of on the chest and because almost all of the Waffen-SS divisions were named as well as numbered, black cuff titles were worn on the lower left sleeve.

The most distinctive item of German combat dress, worn by all ranks, was the steel helmet (*Stahlhelm*). Although its shape gave it the nickname 'coalscuttle', it was actually a very practical item, offering protection to the ears and the neck as well as the skull. A tribute to the soundness of its design is that the modern American combat helmet is virtually identical in shape. The standard M35 helmet was made of steel and weighed around a kilogram depending on size. The supension consisted of an aluminium band covered in leather; this was adjustable to give a comfortable fit as were the black leather chinstraps. A variety of camouflaged helmet covers were also issued, but we shall return to the subject of camouflage later.

Comfortable clothing is very important if a combat soldier is to operate at maximum efficiency, and the Waffen-SS introduced several ideas to enhance that efficiency. These ideas have subsequently been imitated by the armed forces of many other nations.

Over his cotton, aertex or woollen underclothing, the Waffen-SS grenadier wore a grey woollen shirt designed for warmth and ease of movement. Unfortunately, the material had a high wood fibre content, making it scratchy to wear; it also wore out quickly with repeated washing, so later cotton shirts were introduced which were much more practical and popular.

Trousers and tunics were also designed with practicality as well as smartness in mind. Both were made of a wool/rayon mixture, which was extremely hard wearing. The trousers were straight-legged and high-waisted, being supported by braces rather than a belt, although this changed later in the war. The single-breasted tunic, belted at the waist, had four large pockets for carrying personal effects or extra rounds of ammunition.

A variety of field service caps were produced, the most common until 1943 being the sidecap or *Feldmütze*, which was similar in style to those worn by the soldiers of most other armies. In 1943 a peaked cap appeared, the *Einheitsfeldmütze*, which was based upon the mountain troops' ski cap. This was a much more practical piece of headgear, offering protection to the eyes against both rain and sun (men of the Waffen-SS alpine divisions, of course, wore the ski cap or *Bergmütze*).

Paul Hausser wearing the pre-1942 style collar patches of a Gruppenführer. A former staff officer in the army, Hausser had retired in 1932 at the age of 52, joined the SS with the rank of Brigadeführer in 1934 and established the SS-VT Inspectorate in October 1936. He later commanded I SS Panzer Korps in 1943 and Seventh Army in Normandy in 1944. (Bundesarchiv, Koblenz)

▼ ▶ *Two views of the Leibstandarte 'Adolf Hitler' in full parade uniform but without the white belts which later became standard on such occasions. The photo without greatcoats was taken at Tempelhof airfield in Berlin on 24 March 1935. Note the foreground officer is carrying the officer's sabel, or sabre, which was much preferred to the straight-bladed degen and is today a far rarer collector's item. The second photo was taken in Munich on 9 November the same year. The officer in the foreground is Theodor Wisch, who would later command the Leibstandarte 'AH' in Normandy in 1944. (Bundesarchiv, Koblenz)*

Tunics, trousers and hats were also produced in lighter weight materials for tropical wear and, although the Waffen-SS never saw action in North Africa, these were greatly appreciated during the summers in the south of Russia.

For cold weather conditions, the men were issued with a thick woollen calf-length greatcoat, double-breasted for extra protection against the wind. An even thicker version was available for sentries, who needed the extra protection if they were to stay alert. Even these proved inadequate in the arctic conditions of the Russian winter, so by the autumn of 1942 thick, warmly-lined parkas with hoods were being issued. These had drawstrings around the front of the hood and at the waist to help keep the wind out. A sheepskin cap with ear flaps was also introduced.

For footwear, the Waffen-SS started the war wearing the standard German calf-length black leather marching boot (*Marschstiefel*), while officers were entitled to taller riding boots (*Reitstiefel*). Experience with frostbite in Russia led to the introduction of a felt overboot, as well as thick mittens in place of the standard woollen gloves, which were hopelessly inadequate. As the war progressed a more practical lace-up ankle boot (*Schnürschuhe*) was introduced, based on the mountain troops' climbing boots; these were normally worn with canvas gaiters. They gave greater support to the ankle, enhancing the men's mobility.

A Rottenführer of SS Division 'Reich' in the Balkans, 1941, alongside his SdKfz 221 light armoured car. He wears the SS-pattern Panzer tunic and the tank crew beret with its protective inner 'crash helmet', an item of kit which gradually disappeared as the war progressed in favour of soft caps with or without peaks (Feldmütze and Einheitsmütze). (Bundesarchiv, Koblenz)

Camouflage clothing

Production of all uniform items for the Waffen-SS was carried out at concentration camps, particularly Dachau and Buchenwald. This included the camouflage clothing pioneered by the Waffen-SS and which was their most distinctive trademark. Several examples are shown in the photographs and plates, but because this style of clothing was so important, it is worth looking at more closely.

The Waffen-SS were among the first German units to use what has become known as 'disruptive pattern' clothing, designed to help the men blend in with their background surroundings and make them less visible to their enemies. The idea of camouflage itself is, of course, hardly new, but in the modern sense only dates from the turn of the century when the British Army belatedly decided that red tunics made the men marvellous targets and adopted khaki, a practice which, with variations in shade, was rapidly copied by most other armies. Khaki, or the German field grey-green equivalent, are practical, neutral shades, but the Waffen-SS decided this was not going far enough. What was needed was a form of garment to allow the men to blend in not just with different types of countryside, but with seasonal changes in the coloration of grass and foliage.

From the very outbreak of war in September 1939 most Waffen-SS combat troops wore a loose, thigh-length pullover smock over their service tunic. Made of a rayon/cotton mixture, it was generously cut for ease of movement, and could be pulled tight at the waist with a drawstring, offering a degree of extra protection against the wind. The collarless head opening also had a drawstring, as did the cuffs, emphasising the baggy appearance which was quite deliberate and a further form of camouflage in itself.

Early pattern smocks had two chest vents to allow the wearer to reach the pockets in his tunic underneath, but it was soon found that this was impossible when webbing was worn, as it had to be, over the smock, so they were discontinued. Loops were also frequently sewn to the shoulders, upper arms and helmet cover to allow foliage to be attached as extra camouflage.

The smocks were reversible, and printed in a variety of patterns to match the changing seasons: light and dark green for spring, two shades of green and a purplish brown for summer, and three shades of russet and brown for autumn. Quantity fabric printing of such complexity had never been tried before, and special dyes and techniques had to be invented. Early smocks were screen printed, but because this took time, especially since the smocks also had to be waterproofed, later versions were machine printed. The patterns were carefully designed to break up the wearer's outline, with small hard-edged splodges of colour outlined in contrasting colours, so that a man standing still in a wood or hedgerow became virtually invisible. There were four basic patterns used as the war progressed, which for convenience are generally referred to as 'plane tree', 'palm tree', 'oakleaf' and 'pea', although none gave significantly greater camouflage protection than the others, so the reasons for the changes seem to have been merely experimental.

Festooned with stick grenades (Stielgranaten), a young NCO of the 'Der Führer' Regiment, Division 'Das Reich', shows the snow camouflage smock and helmet cover improvised from sheets during the first winter of the Russian campaign, before proper reversible camouflage clothing became available. (Bundesarchiv, Koblenz)

The same camouflage being worn by a pipe-smoking soldier of the same regiment in November 1941 during the drive on Moscow. The man beside him wears a mottle camouflage smock over his greatcoat. Horses came into their own for reconnaissance duties in Russia, but it must not be forgotten that the entire German army was still predominantly 'horse-drawn' throughout most of the war, despite mechanisation. (Bundesarchiv, Koblenz)

In 1942 work began in designing a new uniform for the Waffen-SS grenadier. The result was the M43 drill camouflage uniform. This consisted of a single-breasted jacket and trousers in a rayon mixture, camouflage printed on one side only, the coloration being predominantly dull yellow with green and brown splodges. The M44 suit which followed the M43 was made of coarse herringbone twill which was not as warm. The waterproof qualities of the M44 were also inferior to the M43. The introduction of the M44 field uniform marked the final stage in the simplification and deterioration of the dress of Germany's armed forces.

By 1944, shortages of materials and the need to make economies forced the German Army and the Waffen-SS to adopt a different type of tunic and trousers. The M44 field blouse (Feldbluse) was short-waisted, closely resembling the British Army's battledress blouse. It was made from Zeltbahn material for cheapness, and was distinctly shoddy in ap-

pearance and less warm than earlier tunics. The accompanying trousers were also waist length and tighter fitting, being held up with a belt instead of braces.

The Zeltbahn itself had been developed by the Army, but was adopted by the Waffen-SS. It was a simple triangle of material printed in camouflage colours which could be worn as a poncho in wet weather. The edges had holes for drawstrings, and three or more Zeltbahns could be tied together to form a pup tent. When not in use, it was carried rolled on the back along with the grenadier's other personal equipment, examples of which can be seen in the plates.

EQUIPMENT

The basis for all field equipment was a set of adjustable black leather 'Y' straps which passed from the front of the waistbelt either side of the chest and over the shoulders, converging on a steel ring between the shoulder blades. From this ring a single strap joined to the belt at the centre of the back. The waistbelt itself carried three leather ammunition pouches for the Kar 98 rifle either side of the buckle. The pouches themselves were made as units of three,

and clipped to the 'D' rings which fixed the 'Y' harness to the belt.

Full infantry kit, the M39 pack, was rarely worn in combat by Waffen-SS grenadiers as they were principally shock troops, lightly equipped for mobility and going into action carrying a minimal amount of equipment. When worn—as on the march prior to an engagement—the pack harness was also attached directly to the 'D' rings and to the top of the frontal straps at roughly collarbone level by means of press studs, passing round the waist and under the armpits. To this network was first fixed a canvas backpack, approximately square in shape, which contained the man's washing kit, toothbrush, rifle-cleaning gear, field rations, tent pegs, a length of rope and spare clothing. His mess tin kit was strapped to the back of the pack and his *Zeltbahn* or greatcoat wrapped around its top and sides in a neat but heavy roll. The weight of full kit made it impractical for it to be carried in combat.

Entrenching tools and bayonets were another matter, and formed part of the assault kit. The

◀ *The rigours of the Russian winters saw a wide variety of warm combat clothing being worn. These almost knee-length parkas in a mouse-grey colour were unique to the Waffen-SS and produced by Oswald Pohl's Wirtschafts* VervaltungsHauptAmt *(WVHA, or economic administration department) using concentration camp labour. This photo was taken in Kharkov in March 1943. (Bundesarchiv, Koblenz)*

◀ *Soft sheepskin caps with ear/neck flaps were introduced for tank crews by the second winter in Russia. These had black wool linings on to which the death's head device or national eagle would be pinned. Interestingly, the 'tankie' on the left wears the infantry assault badge. (Bundesarchiv, Koblenz)*

◀ Issue clothing was seldom enough given the excessively low temperatures, and the man on the left here looks as though he can barely move, with camouflage smock belted over a fur or sheepskin coat presumably 'borrowed' from a Russian farmer. In fact, during the winters, the whole of the German armed forces looked more like a collection of scavengers from second-hand shops than anything else. The man on the right wears the standard rubberised motorcyclist's coat and has a scarf wrapped round his head underneath his field cap and goggles. (Bundesarchiv, Koblenz)

▼ Going to the other extreme, the men of the Leibstandarte 'AH' were issued with tropical tunics and solar topees during the invasion of Greece. Note the monogram insignia on the shoulder boards. (Bundesarchiv, Koblenz)

entrenching tool was a simple wooden-handled spade carried in a leather case on the left hip, suspended from the waistbelt. Early versions were square-bladed and did not have a folding handle, while later versions had a triangular point which made a useful improvised weapon, as well as a hinged stock. The harness for both types involved a folding leather three-sided sheath for the blade, the first pattern being secured by a looped leather strap around the top of the handle, the latter by both horizontal and vertical buckled straps.

The bayonet and scabbard were usually strapped to the back of the first pattern entrenching tool; they could, of course, be worn attached simply to the waistbelt, in between the ammunition pouches and the entrenching tool for quick and easy access. This was necessary with the second pattern spade arrangement because it was awkward to get at the spade without first removing the bayonet.

To counterbalance this array, the grenadier carried a canvas bread bag slung from his waistbelt on his right hip. This carried provisions, his field cap when bareheaded or wearing his helmet, and any other oddments which would not fit in elsewhere. The bag itself had two metal rings on its outer straps, one of which was used to attach the kidney-shaped water canteen. The grey-painted fluted metal gas-mask container was not attached to the webbing, but slung around the neck on a canvas strap. It could be in a canvas sack with or without a gas cape. The widespread use of gas was never a serious threat and the gasmask case rapidly became a convenient container for a variety of personal items, particularly those which needed to be kept dry, such as tobacco.

When going into combat, the grenadier would abandon much of the above kit and substitute a canvas 'A' frame, leaving his pack and greatcoat in a truck or dugout and retaining just his mess kit, water bottle, *Zeltbahn* (optional, depending on the weather), bread bag (probably stuffed with grenades instead of rations), entrenching tool and bayonet. The Waffen-SS were flexible in deciding what should be carried into action, but regulations stipulated that the gasmask container was not optional.

WEAPONS

Grenadiers equipped with submachine-guns or, later, assault rifles, did not wear the Kar 98 ammunition pouches on the front of their waistbelts. Instead, they wore two sets of elongated triple pouches in leather or canvas for their weapon's magazines. These were slanted sideways because of their length, clearing the top of the thighs so as not to get in the way when a man was running. Members of machine-gun crews carried no ammunition pouches, but were instead equipped with holstered automatic pistols for self-defence. In fact, within the Waffen-SS as a whole, the carrying of a personal weapon such as a pistol or a submachine-gun in addition to or instead of the issue rifle became something of a cachet.

A pistol is really of little value in a combat situation, having limited range and accuracy, but being small can be carried conveniently by personnel in armoured fighting vehicles, as can SMGs, whereas a rifle would be too unwieldy. However, a pistol is a great morale-booster and a single man so armed can often force the surrender of several opponents if they are shocked and demoralised, as happened quite often in France and during the early period of the advance into Russia. A pistol is also a last defence against capture, and soldiers of the Waffen-SS in

Russia became well aware that a bullet was generally preferable to the latter fate. Pistols and submachine-guns are also useful in close-quarter fighting, as when clearing a building, in dense woods where it is difficult to use a longer-barrelled weapon, or in trench fighting. (In fact, Hugo Schmeisser designed the world's first true submachine-gun, the MP 18, specifically for trench warfare.) Finally, pistols are also symbols of authority and hence would normally be worn by officers and military policemen as a standard part of their uniform.

The most common pistols in service in 1939–40 were the famous 9 mm P 08 Luger and the more modern P 38 Walther, which was put into production in 1938 to replace the former weapon, being cheaper to manufacture. It was also a more practical design, with a lock to prevent accidental firing even with the safety switch 'off'. This was much appreciated by the troops, because there had been several accidents with the Luger when it was field-stripped with a round accidentally left in the chamber. The Walther, on the other hand, even had a pin indicator which could be felt in total darkness and which showed if there was a round 'up the spout'. In fact, the Walther P 38 was such a good weapon that Oberführer Heinrich Gartner, head of the Waffen-SS Procurement Office, tried unsuccessfully to divert all production to the Waffen-SS.

In the early years, the Waffen-SS experienced great difficulty in acquiring the weapons it needed due to the Army's opposition to its growth. Here, men of the 'Totenkopf' Division have nothing better than a captured French 4.7 cm Puteaux anti-tank gun (given the designation Pak 181/183(f) in German service). (Bundesarchiv, Koblenz)

Weariness plainly stamped on his face, a Leibstandarte 'AH' NCO leads his platoon during the invasion of France, June 1940. Hanging from the front of his belt in its leather straps is the wooden holster/stock of a C/96 'broomhandle' Mauser, the first true automatic pistol with a self-loading magazine. It was produced in 7.63 as well as 9 mm calibre and, in the hands of a marksman, could be sighted for up to 1,000 m (1,094 yd), although it would rarely have been used at that sort of range. (Fred Stephens)

Waffen-SS officers were frequently seen equipped with the smaller Walther PP or PPK. Being designed for police use, they were easily concealed, for example at the small of the back, and could be missed in anything other than a thorough body search. The same could not be said for one of the Waffen-SS grenadier's other most popular weapons, the 9 mm C 96 Mauser. Popularly known as the 'broomhandle' Mauser because of the shape of its grip, this ingenious handgun remains one of the finest combat weapons ever made and has become a valued collector's item.

While the Luger and Walther P 38 had eight-round box magazines, could only be fired single-shot and had an effective combat range of little more than 25 yards, the Mauser could take a 20-round magazine, be fired fully automatic like a submachine-gun (or, in German parlance, machine pistol), and had a range of up to 1,000 yards. To enable it to be fired at this range, it had an ingenious hollow wooden stock which doubled as its holster and could also accommodate cleaning tools. Unfortunately, when fired in the fully automatic mode, the Mauser was impossible to aim accurately because of the sharp barrel rise, but

the hail of lead it spouted was guaranteed to send opponents diving for cover . . .

The latter is one of the chief attributes of all submachine-guns. The Waffen-SS used several types of these, but had a definite preference for some over others. In 1940 there were four basic types, the 9 mm MPE (see caption, Plate C1), MP 28, MP 34/35 and MP 38, with the MP 40 just coming into service. All were short-barrelled, with 20- or 32-round box magazines, a high rate of fire and an effective combat range of around 150 yards. However, the Waffen-SS preferred the old MP 28 to the more modern designs because of its superior manufacturing quality and because its magazine slotted into the side of the receiver instead of underneath it. This meant it could be fired from the prone position much more easily. The same was true of the MP 34 and MP 35 produced by the Danish Bergmann company, which had been taken over following the occupation of

◀ *Clearer view of the MP 28 being carried by an Untersturmführer of an unidentified SS Panzer unit. Because of its compact size (only 32 in/ 815 mm including the wooden stock) it was a popular weapon amongst AFV crews. While the* *army preferred the MP 38 and MP 40, the Waffen-SS much appreciated the older but more robust and reliable MP 28 and Bergmann MP 35 and, indeed, took over the entire production of the latter. (Bundesarchiv, Koblenz)*

◀ *This was a standard way of using the 7.92 mm MG 34 (and MG 42) machine-gun during urban battles, although what these two men from 'Das Reich' are laughing about is anyone's guess . . . (Bundesarchiv, Koblenz)*

▶ *The Waffen-SS also made extensive use of captured Russian weapons, such as the PPSh 41 submachine-gun carried by the NCO on the right. (Bundesarchiv, Koblenz)*

Denmark in April 1940 (a campaign in which the Waffen-SS did not take part). The Waffen-SS, short of weapons at the time because of restrictions imposed by the Army (51), were delighted to be allowed to take over the entire production of the Bergmann SMGs, making this weapon uniquely their own.

Other extremely popular non-German weapons used by the Waffen-SS included the 9 mm Browning Hi-Power automatic pistol manufactured by Fabrique Nationale in Belgium. This had a 13-round magazine, making it a much more effective combat weapon than a Luger or Walther, as well as having a more comfortable grip. After the invasion of the Soviet Union in June 1941, captured Russian PPD and PPSh submachine-guns were also pressed into service in large numbers. Home-grown submachine-guns were generally reserved for junior officers and NCOs rather than the rank and file.

While submachine-guns were popular with the Waffen-SS, the principal weapon used by them up to 1943–44 was the German Army's standard 7.92 mm Kar 98 rifle, a traditional breech-loader with a five-round magazine sharing almost identical character-

An SS sniper armed with a Mauser 7.92 mm Kar 98k carbine fitted with telescopic sight. Although designated a carbine and given the suffix 'k' for kurz (short), the Kar 98k's barrel was less than two inches shorter than that of the British and American army's standard Lee-Enfield No 4 Mk I and Springfield M1903, at 23.6 in/600 mm. It was a popular and accurate weapon with a five-round box magazine. Note sand/dust goggles pushed back on helmet. (Bundesarchiv, Koblenz)

istics with the British Lee-Enfield and the American Springfield. Later, the grenadiers eagerly seized the new MP 43/StG 44 assault rifle. The world's first true assault rifle, combining the traditional rifle's virtue of range and accuracy with a submachine-gun's high rate of fire, this had been introduced after combat experience had shown that most firefights took place at under 400 yards.

The Waffen-SS placed great emphasis on laying down saturation firepower, so tried wherever possible to have a greater concentration of heavy support weapons—machine-guns and mortars—than was Army practice. German industry provided two particularly fine weapons for this purpose, the 7.92 mm MG 34 and MG 42. Rightly regarded as the best machine-guns ever made, these had a phenomenal rate of fire and the further advantage of being able to use 75-round saddle drum magazines in place of conventional belts.

Other weapons available to the grenadiers included 'egg' and 'stick' hand grenades; antipersonnel and anti-armour mines and rifle grenades; 5 cm and 8 cm mortars; and flamethrowers. The 5 and 8 cm mortars were later supplemented by 12 cm mortars after experience in Russia had shown the need for a weapon capable of throwing a heavier round to greater range.

At the beginning of the war the infantry had no effective weapons against enemy tanks. In the 1939–40 campaigns this did not matter too much, because French and British tanks were poorly deployed and rarely a threat. In Russia things were totally different, and in response to demand from the front-line troops Dr Heinrich Langweiler devised a

The MG 42 mounted on an SdKfz 251 half-track armoured personnel carrier during the battle of Kursk in July 1943. This, the finest general-purpose machine-gun ever produced, is still in service with the Bundeswehr in only slightly modified form as the 7.62 mm MG 3. The strain of battle is clearly evident on the men's faces. (Bundesarchiv, Koblenz)

very simple but extremely effective weapon capable of stopping any tank then in existence. The *Panzerfaust* ('armour fist') was a single shot weapon comprising a hollow charge warhead expelled from a simple metal tube. The fin-stabilised grenade only had a range of 30 m, requiring nerves of steel to use, but could penetrate 140 mm of armour plate. Subsequently, both range and armour penetration were improved and the *Panzerfaust* was so successful that production peaked at 200,000 units a month.

The second infantry anti-tank weapon, introduced during 1943, was the *Panzerschreck* ('armour battleaxe'). Essentially a copy of American bazookas captured in Tunisia, it was a hollow tube firing a solid fuel rocket with an 88 mm hollow charge warhead. Because the diameter of a hollow charge warhead is the critical factor in determining armour penetration, it was a far more effective weapon than the 60 mm bazooka, and could penetrate 100 mm of armour plate. At 120 m its range was better than that of the *Panzerfaust*. The weapon's only drawbacks were that the flare of the rocket launch gave the operator's position away to the enemy, so he had to be prepared to roll away rapidly to avoid retribution. In addition

the operator had to wear a gasmask to protect his face from the backblast. Subsequently, a small shield incorporating a sight was added. In action, the *Panzerschreck* was crewed by two men, operator and loader, who both normally carried three of the fin-stabilised rockets on their 'A' frame harness.

MANUFACTURE AND MAINTENANCE

As already noted, all Waffen-SS uniforms (other than those tailored privately) were produced in the concentration camps. The German Jewish community included a large number of skilled tailors and seamstresses, and although they were denied all civil rights, it was not the SS Economic Administration Department's policy to let their talents go to waste. (Printing of the actual camouflage material was carried out by specialist private contractors, however.) In the field, each Waffen-SS soldier was issued with needle and thread to effect running repairs, while men who had been cobblers in civilian life found their own talents in demand from their comrades-in-arms who needed their boots re-soled.

Weapons, of course, were manufactured in factories and there is little point in describing the details of these processes. In the field, each man had hand tools (screwdriver, spanner, etc) and cleaning materials for his personal weapons, while more drastic repairs were carried out in mobile field workshops following closely behind the front line.

PSYCHOLOGY AND TRAINING

Before looking at the training which all Waffen-SS infantrymen had to go through, it is important to look at the reasons men enlisted in the Waffen-SS in the first place, rather than the army; and at the factors which made them such tough and often fanatical fighters, earning themselves that description, 'soldiers of destruction'.

Good detail study of a flamethrower team preparing for action. The German army used four basic designs, the Models 35, 40, 41 and 42. The first was very heavy and rapidly replaced by the lighter 40 and 41 (shown here). These all used gas tanks to propel the flammable petrol/gel mixture, but this system proved unable to stand up to the rigours of the Russian winter so the 42 utilised propellant cartridges instead. Flamethrowers are universally hated by the soldiers of all nations and the mere threat of their use has often proved sufficient to force the defenders of a strongpoint to surrender. (Bundesarchiv, Koblenz)

The principal difference between the men who volunteered for the Waffen-SS and those who went into other branches of the armed forces lay in the oath they had to swear, affirming total loyalty to the person of Adolf Hitler rather than to the State. It went as follows and is a key factor in understanding the psychology of the Waffen-SS soldier:

'I swear to thee Adolf Hitler
As Führer and Chancellor of the German Reich
Loyalty and bravery.
I vow to thee and to the superiors whom thou shalt appoint
Obedience unto death
So help me God.'

What, then, did motivate a man to join the Waffen-SS and swear such an oath, rather than going into the regular army? There are many individual answers. For example, the later Kommando leader Otto Skorzeny originally wanted to join the Luftwaffe, but opted for the Waffen-SS instead when he found out that his height would preclude him from serving as aircrew. But more often the answer was simple ambition and the desire to belong to an élite. After the reintroduction of conscription in 1935, the Army's standards were obviously lowered. (Prior to this, the Reichswehr had been restricted to a mere 100,000 men, which meant that recruiting officers could pick and choose.) An ambitious man who realised his own limitations would, quite naturally, prefer to be a big fish in a small pond rather than a small fish in a large one.

Army leaders also realised this, and exercised tight controls over the number of men eligible for national service whom they would permit to join the SS. Seeing what was happening, Hitler put the entire SS on to the police rather than the Army budget. This gave the Army more money to play with and helped reduce their animosity towards the growth of the SS, an animosity based on the fact that the Army was traditionally the sole arms bearer for the State and undiminished by the fact that the prewar Waffen-SS was a relatively tiny organisation.

There were two other significant differences between volunteers for the Waffen-SS and for the Army. Although the SS physical requirements were higher (see below), their educational ones were lower. Nearly half of all Waffen-SS recruits had received only minimal schooling, and officer candidates especially were accepted with far lower academic qualifications than their counterparts in the Army. This, of course, made them more amenable both to the tight discipline and to ideological indoctrination. (It should be noted that these remarks apply only to the Waffen-SS and not to, for example, the SD—the SS security service headed by Reinhard Heydrich—which attracted a high proportion of young lawyers and administrators with university degrees.)

The other difference is that the majority of volunteers for the Waffen-SS came from rural areas, whereas the bulk of the Army's ranks were composed of city dwellers. This process of natural selection vindicated itself later in a way which seems rather surprising, until you remember that fifty-odd years ago rural living conditions were far more primitive and, literally, closer to the earth than they are today. Thus it soon became apparent, particularly in Russia, that the majority of men in the Waffen-SS divisions were more comfortable living in the field, and more adept at field- and woodcraft, than their urban comrades-in-arms. Since one of the basic requirements of a soldier is to survive in order to be able to fight, this was a not insignificant asset.

Recruits for the Waffen-SS—at least in the early days, before wartime demands forced a relaxation of standards—had to satisfy stringent physical and moral conditions. 'Sepp' Dietrich, the commander of the Leibstandarte 'Adolf Hitler'—Hitler's SS bodyguard—wanted mature men rather than pimply teenagers, so only recruited from those aged between 23 and 35, at least five feet eleven inches tall, and in peak physical condition. No man was accepted if he

Training in the Waffen-SS placed high emphasis on physical standards of attainment which are only paralleled today by those of élite units such as paratroopers or marines.

These men are officer candidates at Bad Tölz, one of the two specialist training schools overseen by Paul Hausser; the other was at Braunschweig. (Bundesarchiv, Koblenz)

When Hitler assumed power in 1933, a rush of waverers—the 'March Violets', who had previously sat on the political fence—practically fell over each other in their enthusiasm to join the NSDAP, the SA and the SS. Membership of the SA reached an incredible three million, while the ranks of the SS swelled to some 50,000. The SA, led by the portly homosexual Ernst Röhm, saw themselves as the true national revolutionary army, a fact which alarmed Hitler, who began to regard them as a threat to his own power. Accordingly, in June 1934 he used the black-uniformed troops of the Leibstandarte as well as men from Theodore Eicke's Totenkopfverbände to arrest and execute many of the SA leaders, including Röhm himself. Thus emasculated, the SA would never again pose a threat. But Himmler had a similar problem within the SS itself, because the rush of newcomers to their ranks were not of the old calibre. So, over the next few months he initiated a ruthless house cleaning process, expelling from the SS large numbers of 'Johnny-come-latelies' on grounds of alcoholism, criminal records, homosexuality or the inability to prove pure 'Aryan' ancestry, thus restoring to the survivors the status of an élite.

Initial enlistment was 25 years for officers, 12 for

Officer candidates on the assault course at Bad Tölz. The lack of heavy equipment is deliberate, because the Waffen-SS placed emphasis on light infantry tactics rather more than did the army. (Bundesarchiv, Koblenz)

had a criminal record, and he had to be able to prove pure 'Aryan' ancestry with no 'taint' of Jewish blood. Until the need to replace casualties forced him to relax his own standards, Dietrich would not even accept a man into the Leibstandarte if he had a single tooth filled. He was determined that the regiment would be the toughest, fittest and most highly disciplined unit in the Führer's service, and right to the very end it attracted the cream of volunteers for the Waffen-SS.

The army also often accused the Waffen-SS of being 'unnaturally' aggressive, despite the fact that controlled aggression is the soldier's profession. Here, a couple of recruits slog it out in a simulated trench assault designed to teach the tactics of both attack and defence. Much of the success of the premier Waffen-SS formations had its foundations laid in such realistic training. (Bundesarchiv, Koblenz)

NCOs and four for other ranks, and candidates were only permitted to apply for officer training after serving at least two years in the ranks, unless they had previous equivalent service in the Army. Despite these lengthy periods, and despite the tough physical, racial and moral entry requirements, there was no shortage of volunteers. Unfortunately, in the early days, what the Waffen-SS badly lacked was experienced officers, and this was to be a contributory factor in their high casualty rate during the 1940 campaign.

Initial training was carried out in depots outside each regiment's home town; for example, the 'Totenkopf' Division was based at Dachau, Standarte 'Deutschland' was at Munich while 'Germania' was at Hamburg. But to begin with there was no consistency, so in 1936 Himmler created a Waffen-SS Inspectorate headed by a highly experienced former Army officer, Paul Hausser. Brand new officer training schools were built at Bad Tölz and Braunschweig with light and airy barracks and classrooms.

◀ *Marksmanship was rigorously 'encouraged', and drilling in shooting and weapons' care was so thorough that everything became automatic, almost instinctive. Here, cadets practise their skills on the butts at Bad Tölz. (Bundesarchiv, Koblenz)*

Hausser was helped in initiating the training programme by two men in particular: Felix Steiner and Cassius Freiherr von Montigny.

Steiner had been a member of a *Stosstruppe*, or assault troop, during the First World War, and wanted to instil the Waffen-SS with a similar style and élan. These assault troops had consisted of small bodies of volunteers armed to the teeth not only with the first submachine-guns but also with improvised weapons such as clusters of grenades wrapped around a single stick, shields like a medieval knight, and entrenching tools with their edges sharpened like razors. They were true light infantry, just as the Waffen-SS grenadiers were to become, going into action in daring trench raids unencumbered by the usual weight of kit, just carrying weapons, ammunition and water bottles. This, Steiner decided, would be the style of the SS; let the Army provide the cannon fodder . . .

Montigny, a First World War U-boat skipper, had similarly strong ideas on discipline. Between them, he and Steiner were determined to create a force of men who would be tough, ruthless and self-disciplined, and to a large degree they succeeded. What they also created was a force of men who were almost recklessly brave and totally callous where human life was concerned, factors which were to have repercussions on the battlefield in the form of a number of appalling atrocities.

The training programme evolved for the 'Deutschland' and 'Germania' Standarten was broadly followed by the Leibstandarte, although, because of their ceremonial duties, the men in the latter regiment had to endure a great deal more 'spit and polish'. Similarly, the same programme was followed in only slightly modified form when Theodore Eicke began the transformation of part of the Totenkopfverbände into the 'Totenkopf' Division.

The normal day's routine began at 6 am with the recruits dressed in PE kit being put through an hour's callisthenics before breakfast, which usually consisted of porridge and mineral water. (This was partly due to Himmler's own dietary fanaticism and partly to the fact that the SS Economic Department had the monopoly on both these products!) After breakfast, the men changed into fatigues or service dress, depending on the day's programme. Of all the aspects of military training weapons training, received the greatest emphasis. First the men had to learn how to strip, clean and reassemble their rifles. This took place in the classroom, the instructor using a large wall chart showing the weapon in exploded view to explain the function of each part. Then the men had

◀ *On campaign, the training shows its value. Despite their exhaustion at the end of a day's march during the invasion of the West in May/June 1940, these men clean their weapons before the next day's struggle. The bedroom slippers are strictly non-regulation! (Bundesarchiv, Koblenz)*

▶ *Such attention to detail paid dividends, and the men of the three principal SS formations involved in Fall Gelb ('Case Yellow') had not only the satisfaction of seeing a job done well, but of witnessing the Inspector-General of the SS, Paul Hausser, pinning medals on practically everyone who would stand still for long enough . . . (Bundesarchiv, Koblenz)*

to practise on their own rifles, repeating the process endlessly, day after day, until they could do it blindfold. They were shown how to clear blockages and effect simple field repairs. Then it was out on to the firing butts for target practice at steadily increasing ranges. Those who proved 'gun shy' or who simply had no aptitude despite patient encouragement were eased out into administrative or other tasks, because the SS obviously needed signallers, clerks, cooks and so on as much as any other army does.

Once the men were familiar with their weapons they would begin learning infantry assault techniques, charging at sandbags with fixed bayonets. The instructors put great emphasis on aggression, constantly stressing fierceness in the attack both as a means of winning battles quickly and of minimising casualties. To this end the men were taught the techniques of unarmed combat by qualified martial arts instructors and, later, when they were sufficiently skilled to be able to practise against each other without causing injury, they would fight mock battles

Apart from infantry, cavalry, Panzer and Panzergrenadier divisions, the Waffen-SS also incorporated five mountain divisions (plus another two which only existed on paper), the 6th Gebirgs Division 'Nord', 7th Freiwilligen (Volunteer) Division 'Prinz Eugen', 13th Waffen Gebirgs Division of the SS 'Handschar' (Kroatische Nr 1), 21st Waffen Gebirgs Division of the SS 'Skanderberg' (Albanische Nr 1) and 24th Waffen Gebirgs Division of the SS 'Karstjäger', the latter composed of Italian fascists. These two men strapping up their equipment prior to scaling a rock face are from the 'Prinz Eugen' Division which was formed under Artur Phleps from Hungarian, Romanian and Yugoslavian volunteers in 1942. (Bundesarchiv, Koblenz)

using rifle and bayonet, or just the bayonet on its own. To further encourage aggression, boxing featured as a major part of the curriculum, helping the men to get over the instinctive fear of being hurt and teaching them that getting your own blow in first is the best way of avoiding just that.

In fact, sport played a major part in the Waffen-SS training programme, much more so than in the Army. All forms of field and track sports were encouraged, not just for relaxation as in the Army but as part of the training itself, as a means of enhancing physical fitness and reflexes. And, of course, there were endless route marches and cross-country runs, both with and without full kit, to develop stamina and endurance.

Before getting out into the air again the men would have a hearty midday meal, followed by a 'make and mend' session during which barracks were scoured, boots cleaned, uniforms pressed and repaired and any other chores attended to. In the evening, the recruits could read, write letters, play cards or chess—the latter game being particularly encouraged because of the way it helps develop both logical thinking and mental flexibility. Those recruits lucky enough to have secured a pass could go into town so long as they first passed a rigorous examination by the duty officer of the guard.

So far, apart from those already noted, there was little difference between the training of a Waffen-SS grenadier and his Army counterpart. What they had to endure additionally was formal lectures at least three times a week covering the policies of the NSDAP and intense indoctrination in SS philosophy, particularly the theories of racial superiority which destined them to rule over the 'untermensch'—the so-called 'sub-human' Jews, gypsies, Freemasons and communists. Slavs were rapidly added to the list once the invasion of the Soviet Union became a reality, but shortly afterwards the SS hierarchy began changing its mind. Latvians, Lithuanians and Estonians, it was decided, were not 'Slav' but essentially 'Germanic'. So, it turned out, were Ukrainians, Azerbaijanis and anyone else who hated Moscow, almost regardless of their origins, because casualties created such a huge manpower demand.

Into this melting pot would also flow Indians and Palestinians, as well as men from every European

Fine study of a 'Totenkopf' NCO in Russia, summer 1941, wearing appropriately coloured camouflage smock and helmet cover (without loops), standard 8 × 50 binoculars, leather map case and Luger P/o8 holster. An MP 28/II submachine-gun is slung across his back. (Bundesarchiv, Koblenz)

country (Britain not excepted), who all swore variants of the basic Waffen-SS oath and adherence to its motto, 'Meine Ehre heist Treue', which can be translated either way as 'my loyalty is my honour', or 'honour is my loyalty'. Thus, its initial idealism diffused, the Waffen-SS actually became a polyglot organisation whose members fell far short of the standards demanded by Hausser, Dietrich, Steiner and the remainder of the 'old guard'.

While those original standards were high, they did not go far enough as far as Himmler was

A despatch rider of the 'Totenkopf' Division being given directions by an officer whose tunic is so elegant it must have been privately tailored. Note the loop sewn into the side of the motorcyclist's helmet cover to take camouflage 'garnish'. The bike itself is a 350 cc BMW R35. (Bundesarchiv, Koblenz)

concerned. He was virulently anti-Church (Theodore Eicke was even more so), even though he adopted many practical Jesuit principles in the organisation and creed of the SS, to such an extent that Hitler called him 'my Ignatius Loyola' after the founder of the Society of Jesus. This anti-Christian campaign was never even nearly wholly successful and almost half the men in the original Waffen-SS regiments remained churchgoers despite peer criticism and insult (the figure was only 31 per cent in the Totenkopfverbände).

What the ideological lectures aimed at producing were men who firmly believed in their own destiny as missionaries of the new 'Aryan' order which would rule the world. They were thoroughly indoctrinated in Nazi philosophy, so that they would know what they were fighting for. While many believed in this, others were more cynical and believed purely that

they were fighting to make their country strong again, as well as forming part of an élite. This, coupled to their allegiance to the Führer, goes most of the way towards accounting for the almost suicidal courage and determination of the Waffen-SS soldier on the battlefield. Certainly, few were taken in by Himmler's SS mythology, based on his readings of early German history reinforced by a mystical belief in reincarnation, in the old pagan Nordic gods and in runic symbolism. Yet, having said that, the award of the SS Totenkopfring—a silver ring with a skull and crossbones on the front and other runic symbols around the sides supposedly reinforcing the bearer's 'psychic' Germanic virtues—was one of the most coveted of all awards. It was not a military decoration like the Iron Cross, but a personal 'thank you' from the Reichsführer-SS, and the rings themselves were supposed to go to the graves with their bearers or be returned; they could not be sold or inherited.

Once the Waffen-SS recruit had survived this basic training and ideological and 'spiritual' indoctrination, he could—like a trainee soldier anywhere—get down to learning more complex tasks. In particular, and more so than in any contemporary armed force before the emergence of the British Commandos and the American Rangers, for example, Steiner and his team of instructors intended that the SS grenadier would be able to handle himself and his weapons competently under any conceivable battlefield situation, by day or night, regardless of terrain or weather. Individual training still continued, but increasingly gave way to unit training, first at the squad level of eight men and gradually broadening out into exercises at company, battalion and regimental level. Finally, full-scale exercises would be held involving the whole of a division.

The only way in which this training differed from the Army's was, as we have seen, in the emphasis on aggression and overwhelming firepower. The Waffen-SS had plenty of the former but, as we shall see later, initially at least were hampered in acquiring the latter. They were in a situation rather like the Army's *Panzerwaffe*—knowing what they wanted, but unable to get enough in sufficient time. This situation changed as the war progressed and Hitler came to place increasing reliance on his Waffen-SS divisions to 'get the job done', giving them priority in the issue of new equipment; but to begin with it was far from true.

At the first two levels, the training programme taught the integration of squad and company support weapons—the machine-guns, mortars, flame-throwers and, later, *Panzerfausts* and *Panzerschrecks*. This involved learning games theory, although it was not described as such at the time. What games theory tells you, for example, is that a bolt-action rifle fired at a one-metre-square target at a range of 200 metres has a seven out of ten probability of hitting, assuming average marksmanship. The same theory tells us that a submachine-gun or assault rifle fired on automatic only has a two in ten probability, and a machine-gun on a bipod mount three in ten. What this does *not* mean is that a machine-gun is less effective than a bolt-action rifle, because the equation does not take into account that a machine-gun can be pouring 500-plus rounds into the same target area in the time it would take to aim about 15 rifle shots. Viewed like this, the machine-gun will get 150 hits on the target, the rifle only ten or so. Now, I am quoting here because I am far from being a mathematician, but increasing the distance beyond 200 metres (assuming

the weapon is capable of doing this) affects its basic accuracy by $A = a (200/D)$, when A is the new base accuracy of the weapon at the increased range, a is the original accuracy figure (eg, seven out of ten) and D is the new distance to the target.

Games theory coupled to empirical research gives many such equations and the Waffen-SS grenadier was hardly expected to learn them, merely how to put them into practice to give the best results depending upon the tactical circumstances. Thus, sometimes a single-shot rifle is the best weapon, sometimes a submachine-gun and sometimes a machine-gun. Small unit tactical training therefore encourages the individual soldier to experiment with different combinations to gain the best results based on his judgement of terrain, weather, visibility, his own men's abilities and the capability and weapons

A brief rest for the crew of a 'Das Reich' PzKpfw III during the battle of Kusk. There is little uniformity of dress apart from the mottle camouflage smocks. One man has field grey trousers and calf-length boots while the others have black trousers and ankle boots; similarly, two wear the grey Feldmütze, *two the black and one an* Einheitsmütze. *(Bundesarchiv, Koblenz)*

Brigadeführer Hermann Fegelein was the first commander of the 8th SS Cavalry Division 'Florian Geyer', and resumed command when 'Willi' Bittrich took over 'Hohenstaufen'. Later, he was appointed to the Führer Headquarters staff. The fact that he was married to Eva Braun's sister Gretl did not save him from execution when he was accused of attempting to flee from Berlin in April 1945. (Bundesarchiv, Koblenz)

casualties it caused. In the long run, however, such exercises certainly *saved* lives, because once they went to war the men of the Waffen-SS were not unnerved by the simple fact of being under return fire. The efficacy of live-firing exercises is proven by their almost universal adoption elsewhere after the Waffen-SS pioneered the way; but at the same time it must be admitted that such training can produce over-confidence, and this could account (along with the inexperienced leadership already noted) for some of the Waffen-SS's heavy casualties during their early campaigns.

Apart from the matter of live firing, Waffen-SS training differed from that of the Army in two other important ways. In the first place, although total discipline was demanded and ruthlessly enforced, training was designed to produce inner discipline and self-reliance. Only a soldier who knows that his 'mates' have been through the same treadmill will trust them, and vice versa. And in the second place, Steiner in particular strove to break down the traditional Prussian barriers between officers and men, encouraging them to talk and exchange ideas as equals when off duty and to address each other as 'kamerad' rather than by rank. This was no easy process, because class distinctions had far from disappeared from the Germany of the 1930s, but the process was helped by the fact that the NSDAP had created a new class of people who were appointed on merit rather than through an accident of birth. This meant that a man like 'Sepp' Dietrich, for example, and others like him who could barely have expected to rise to senior NCO rank in the Army, could become colonels and generals within the Waffen-SS. It was a reversion to Napoleon's old principle of 'a Marshal's baton in every private's knapsack' (on top of which, Hitler fully recognised the truth of one of Napoleon's other adages—'give me enough medals to hand out and I'll win you any battle', and by introducing such awards as the Knights Cross of the Iron Cross had gone a long way towards creating an army which could only be defeated by 'bigger battalions', not by skill).

There was more to the success of the Waffen-SS than this, however. In a very real sense, the men had an esprit de corps more comparable to that of Regular British Army regiments than most German Army ones. Because they were formed as a deliberate élite,

effectiveness of the enemy. Some factors are obvious—that increasing range diminishes accuracy, for example, or that laying down saturation fire will keep your enemy's head down while allowing you to get on with the approach to the objective.

Understanding such basics is fairly simple, putting them into practice effectively a matter of experience, and to give their men that experience Hausser, Steiner and their staffs made great use of live ammunition in exercises, a technique which at the time attracted strong criticism from the Army hierarchy because of the inevitable accidental

recruited and trained as such, and awarded regimental cuff titles, they had a far stronger bond with their parent regiment than an Army conscript did with his. They were also volunteers, emphasising—as in the British Army—their professionalism in their own minds. And they shared the same love of sports, which might seem a minor point, but perhaps is not.

One way in which they definitely differed from the British (or German) Army of the time was in the relationship between officers and enlisted men, not least because every Waffen-SS officer had had to have served at least two years in the ranks or completed equivalent service elsewhere. Officers themselves were positively encouraged to discuss their decisions and orders (after the event, of course, not at the time; no effective military machine can be operated as a democracy). This was designed to enable their men to understand why they were asked to do things in a certain way, and help build confidence in the officers to whom they had sworn 'obedience unto death'. Theodore Eicke, when he began training up the 'Totenkopf' Division at Dachau, went still further, instructing junior officers that they were to take some of their meals in the other ranks' and NCOs' messes, and even introducing suggestion boxes through which his men could leave ideas or air complaints anonymously.

Himmler wanted the Waffen-SS to be a brotherhood, an extended family, and this resulted in the men learning to trust their officers as well as each other, with little of the 'them and us' attitude prevalent in most other armies at the time. Regrettably, these ideals began to break down later, when the Waffen-SS began accepting volunteers from the occupied countries.

Foreign volunteers

This is a subject which really needs deeper investigation than space permits here, but some of the books listed in the bibliography should prove helpful. The first question is why on earth, within weeks of seeing their own countries overrun by the German armed forces, should hundreds of volunteers from Norway, Denmark, Holland and Belgium flock to join the ranks of the Waffen-SS?

Austrians and Czechs were already being absorbed into the SS prior to 1940, both countries having had fairly extensive Nazi parties of their own

The Waffen-SS attracted recruits from all the occupied countries. This Propaganda Company ciné cameraman wears the Norwegian flag on his sleeve, probably denoting a member of Standarte 'Nordland', 5th SS Panzergrenadier (later Panzer) Division 'Wiking'. (Bundesarchiv, Koblenz)

before their almost bloodless take-overs. Besides, the majority of the populations of both countries were essentially 'German', had seen the effects of Hitler's economic miracle, and wanted to take part in the 'great adventure'.

But why the others—particularly before the invasion of Russia gave an excuse to anyone who was anti-communist—should have wanted to join up remains even today something of a mystery. Some I have spoken to have simply shrugged and said the equivalent of 'it seemed a good idea at the time'. What is fascinating is that most are proud of the fact, even after being vilified by their fellow countrymen following their release from internment camp or prison.

Inevitably, some were politically inspired, just as were the Italian blackshirts who continued to fight in SS units after the overthrow of Mussolini and Italy's surrender in 1943. It must be remembered that extreme right-wing, anti-Semitic and anti-

Volunteers did not just come from western Europe. There was warm response to Gottlob Berger's recruiting campaign from men in the Baltic States, occupied by the Soviet Union in 1940, who welcomed the Germans as liberators. Amongst these, the toughest and most disciplined were the Latvians, who formed the 15th and 19th Waffen Grenadier Divisions of the SS (Lettische Nr 1 and Nr 2). They were uniformed identically to other members of the Waffen-SS apart from the distinctive collar patches. (Bundesarchiv, Koblenz)

communist parties were not restricted to Germany, Austria, Spain and Italy in the 1920s and '30s, and even the United Kingdom had its share of similarly-minded fanatics in Oswald Moseley's blackshirt fascist movement.

Politics were only part of the answer, however. Another part was, strangely, the fact of occupation itself. Many men, recognising the sheer military virtuosity of the German armed forces and the ineffectual resistance of their own, were keen to join such a magnificent fighting machine once the opportunity arose—an opportunity which the chief Waffen-SS recruiting officer, Gottlob Berger, was eager to exploit because it expanded his own and Himmler's empire without treading on the toes of the Army. Most people in the occupied countries—to begin with, at least—were also impressed by the smart turn-out and correct behaviour of the occupying forces. Finally, it must be admitted that, like many farm labourers in Germany itself, many enlisted in the Waffen-SS for the same reason that for decades had drawn others into the French Foreign Legion: for adventure, glamour and travel, or to escape from problems at home (it should be noted rather ironically that quite a few Waffen-SS men found sanctuary from postwar prosecution in the Legion . . .).

Most of the early western European foreign volunteers eventually found themselves in either the

'Wiking' or 'Nordland' Divisions, where they discovered that things were not quite as rosy as they had been painted. Their officers were predominantly German, and unfortunately for those like Steiner who were trying to create something like a pan-European precursor of the North Atlantic Treaty Organisation, the new recruits from the occupied countries quickly found that they were regarded as second-class citizens in the Waffen-SS. This was partly because they swore a slightly different oath, partly because their mastery of the German language was often insufficient, leading to misunderstandings, and partly because many German SS officers *did*

TACTICS

Probably the most famous foreign volunteer in the Waffen-SS was the Belgian Rexist leader Léon Degrelle, hero of the battle for the Cherkassy Pocket in February 1944. Here he wears standard army uniform because the Wallonien Brigade which he commanded was not incorporated into the SS as the 28th SS Freiwilligen Panzergrenadier Division 'Wallonien' until later in the year. By this time Degrelle had been awarded the Knights Cross with Oakleaves and promoted to Oberführer. Prior to this he had always, as in this photograph, worn the simple uniform of a private. (Christopher Ailsby Historical Archives)

The basis of German military philosophy at the beginning of the war and through to 1942 remained that of Blitzkrieg ('lightning war'), and was repeated on both the grand and the small scale. Particularly, it must be noted, within the Waffen-SS, with their emphasis on aggression and speed.

Like all successful concepts, that of Blitzkrieg was simplicity itself although it is still often misunderstood, even today. The idea was to mass sufficient force against one sector of the enemy line in order to achieve superiority, break through and *keep moving* as rapidly as possible to keep the enemy off balance while secondary attacks either side of the breakthrough point prevented him from transferring reinforcements. It was this idea of continuous movement with an almost total disregard for flanks which made the Blitzkrieg concept work so well in those early years, since the Germans' opponents were unable to respond quickly enough—despite having an overall superiority in manpower, guns and tanks—to check the tidal wave of men and machines. The 1940 campaign in France and the Low countries is perhaps the best example of these failings.

Blitzkrieg relied upon the *integrated* use of all weapons systems, and was greatly assisted by the fact that German military organisation was built on the modular system, with plug-in replacements. The Waffen-SS used the same principle with élan, but one significant difference did emerge between themselves and the Army. This lay in their loyalty to their parent regiment. An Army soldier, unless he was himself a member of an élite formation such as the 'Grossdeutschland' Division, did not particularly care which unit he fought within. There was no fierce loyalty, by and large, such as existed within the Waffen-SS for their 'own' unit. This made interchange of personnel more difficult, because a man would be reluctant to move to a different regiment (except by the prospect of promotion); so the formation of *ad hoc* battlegroups (Kampfgruppen) was much more rare within the Waffen-SS than within the Army. Men preferred to stay with their own unit even if it had been decimated.

It was inevitable that this feeling should extend down to company and squad level, men who had

regard them as second class and resented their own appointment to command them.

This resulted in many of the volunteers feeling they were being victimised, for example by being given extra duties or docked pay for imaginary transgressions while the German soldiers alongside whom they were soon to be fighting got away scot free with similar offences. Felix Steiner did everything he could to counteract this situation, even to the issuance of standing written instructions, but it did not really improve until the new 'European-Germanic' formations went into combat in Russia. Then the German attitude began to change drastically as the men proved themselves in combat, the 'Wiking' Division in particular ending the war with as fine a combat record as any.

trained together and learned to trust each other trying to stick together because they knew how their comrades thought and acted, what their strong and weak points were. This, again, is true in most armies, but was particularly so in the Waffen-SS and some of the élite formations of other nations. And what it all boils down to tactically is that the men of the Waffen-SS—at whichever structural level you care to pick—acted as a team. The machine-gunners and mortar crews would lay down as high a concentration of firepower as possible, enabling the rest of their section to crawl, or dash where there was cover, towards the objective. Then the grenades would be hurled, the building or trench saturated with gunfire, and the squad would move on, trusting to their companions in flanking units to watch their backs if their own progress had been slower. In this way, small Waffen-SS units often outstripped the main advance of their parent unit by miles, sacrificing security for the speed and surprise of sustained momentum.

A classic example of this is Fritz Klingenberg's almost single-handed capture of the Yugoslav capital of Belgrade during Operation 'Strafe' ('Punishment') in 1941.

During the invasion of Yugoslavia, a young Hauptsturmführer called Fritz Klingenberg particularly distinguished himself. As commander of a company in the 'Reich' Division's reconnaissance battalion, he was determined to reach Belgrade before any other German troops. Commandeering a small boat on 11 April 1941, he took a party of ten men across the Danube, dangerously swollen by the spring rains, marched unopposed into the city and accepted its surrender from the mayor. (Bundesarchiv, Koblenz)

▶ *Light trucks of the 'Reich' Division roll through Belgrade after its surrender. Note the divisional marking on the mudguard and the SS number plate. (Bundesarchiv, Koblenz)*

Hauptsturmführer (Captain) Klingenberg, a graduate from Bad Tölz, was commanding the second company of the 'Reich' Division's motorcycle reconnaissance battalion at the time, and was keenly aware that his unit was flanked by the Army's crack 'Grossdeutschland' Regiment. The result was a race to see who was best, the Army or the Waffen-SS, with Belgrade the winner's prize.

As it turned out, it was rather a race in slow motion, because the spring rains had turned Yugoslavia's largely unpaved roads into a quagmire of glutinous mud in which the motorcycles bogged down all too frequently. Nevertheless, thanks to finding a bridge which had not been demolished over the Vlasecki Canal, Klingenberg and his men managed to reach the pivotal town of Alibuna in front of their rivals during the evening of 11 April. Despite the late hour, they were ordered to push on another 20 km to Pancevo, arriving at midnight.

The following day, despite their exhaustion, Klingenberg forced his men on, but they were hampered by the lack of bridges over the River Tamis, which allowed leading elements of the 'Grossdeutschland' Regiment to catch up with them. Klingenberg's goal on the far side of the swollen rivers Tamis and Danube was tantalisingly in sight, but seemed unreachable until pioneers arrived with rubber assault boats. Klingenberg went out on a personal recce in search of an alternative, and to his delight found an abandoned motor boat. It was in a very dilapidated condition and crossing the rivers in such a craft was fraught with peril, so Klingenberg called for volunteers to accompany him. Almost every man in his company raised their hands, but the boat would only carry a few, and in the end he selected ten of his best.

Crossing the Danube with this tiny task force, Klingenberg marched into Belgrade itself. Astonishingly, there was no resistance, although when Klingenberg reached the German Mission in the city centre he found it besieged by an angry crowd. Klingenberg set up his two machine-guns and the crowd hurriedly dispersed. Inside the Mission, Klingenberg summoned the city's mayor by telephone and demanded his surrender, threatening to call up an air strike if he did not receive immediate obedience. This was pure bluff, because he did not have a radio, but the mayor was not to know this and hastily

Photographed in Russia a few months later, Klingenberg now wears the Knights Cross he was awarded for the capture of Belgrade. He later became commandant at Bad Tölz and was finally given command of the 17th SS Panzergrenadier Division 'Götz von Berlichingen'. He was killed in action in April 1945. (Bundesarchiv, Koblenz)

signed a surrender document. Shortly afterwards, leading elements of the 11th Panzer Division arrived in the city, believing themselves first. Their chagrin, and the celebrations in 'Reich' Division's headquarters when the news was confirmed, can be well imagined. Klingenberg himself was awarded the Knights Cross for his achievement.

This story is illuminating in several respects. It demonstrates the determination of the Waffen-SS to show that they were better than the Army. It shows their will, aggression and audacity. And it is a small-scale example of Blitzkrieg tactics in operation.

Defensive Tactics

As the war progressed, such tactics became increasingly impossible. When Russian resistance stiffened and then turned to the offensive, the Waffen-SS had to acquire new skills. Aggression alone was no longer enough, the lightning strikes and rapid advances no longer feasible. Now the Waffen-SS grenadiers had to learn to endure in the face of an implacable and numerically superior foe whose equipment was in some respects also becoming superior.

It was impossible in Russia, given the vast distances involved, to hold a continuous front line from the Baltic to the Black Sea, so what were known as 'hedgehog' tactics evolved. A division would occupy a cluster of villages, each held in company or battalion strength. In a sense it was like the old infantry 'square' of Napoleonic times designed to repel cavalry. The Russian attacks swirled round the 'hedgehogs' and were fired into from the flanks and rear until they were exhausted. Mere companies of Waffen-SS men held out against attacks by whole divisions. They were not always successful, of course, and there are many instances reminiscent of the French Foreign Legion's stand at Camerone, when, finally out of ammunition, the surviving grenadiers would charge their opponents with fixed bayonets and die to a man. They had, after all, vowed 'obedience unto death'.

During the long retreat from the summer of 1943—by which time the cream of the SS grenadiers, mounted in armoured half-tracks instead of tanks, had been renamed Panzergrenadiers—the Waffen-SS proved itself as skilful in defence as in the attack. Rushed from one trouble spot to another like a mobile fire brigade, they succeeded time and again in stemming the Russian tide and inflicting enormous casualties. But they suffered in turn, and the new cadres of young replacements—the original age limits having been abandoned—were totally unprepared for conditions on the Eastern Front.

TYPICAL ENGAGEMENTS

In one sense there is no such thing as a 'typical' engagement since each has its own unique features. Take the attack on Greece in April 1941, in which the Leibstandarte took part while 'Reich' was heading for Belgrade. Again, the reconnaissance battalion was in its rightful place in the van of the attack. However, they encountered far stiffer opposition from the tough Greek and British Empire troops opposing them, and at one point the battalion, commanded by

A dapper officer of the 'Das Reich' Division during the advance into Russia, summer 1941. He wears the old style officers' peaked cap and riding breeches tucked into knee boots, and has the neck of his camouflage smock well open to display his Knights Cross. (Bundesarchiv, Koblenz)

1: Hauptsturmführer, LSSAH,
30 June 1934
2: 9mm Luger P08 automatic
pistol (cutaway to show
internal mechanism)

A

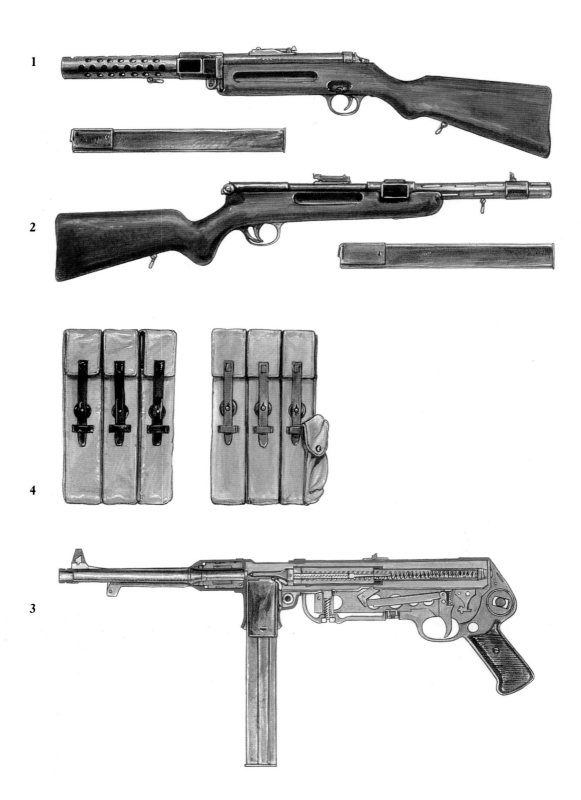

B

5

7   **8**   **6**

1: 9mm Schmeisser (Haenel) MP28 submachine-gun
2: 9mm Bergmann MP34/35 submachine-gun
3: 9mm MP38/40 submachine-gun (cut away to show internal mechanism)
4: Leather and canvas MP38/MP40 magazine pouches
5: 7.92 mm MP43 assault rifle
6: Leather and canvas MP43 magazine pouches
7: M1939 Eiergranate
8: M1924 Stielhandgranate
9: 7.92mm MG42 machine-gun

9

2a

2b

3

1

1: Rifleman's 'Y' straps with 'D' rings and belt
2a: NCO and other ranks' belt buckle
2b: Officer's belt buckle
3: M1931 field flask and drinking cup

8

9

C

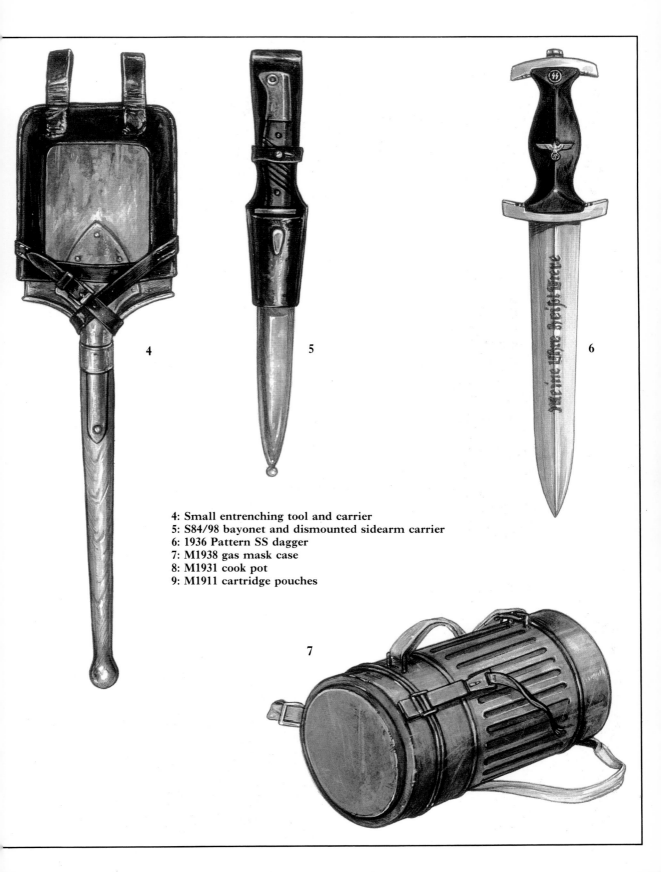

4: Small entrenching tool and carrier
5: S84/98 bayonet and dismounted sidearm carrier
6: 1936 Pattern SS dagger
7: M1938 gas mask case
8: M1931 cook pot
9: M1911 cartridge pouches

4

5

6

7

1: Unterscharführer,
1st SS-VT Standarte
'Deutschland',
France, June 1940
2: 9mm Mauser C96 automatic pistol
(cutaway to show
internal mechanism)

D

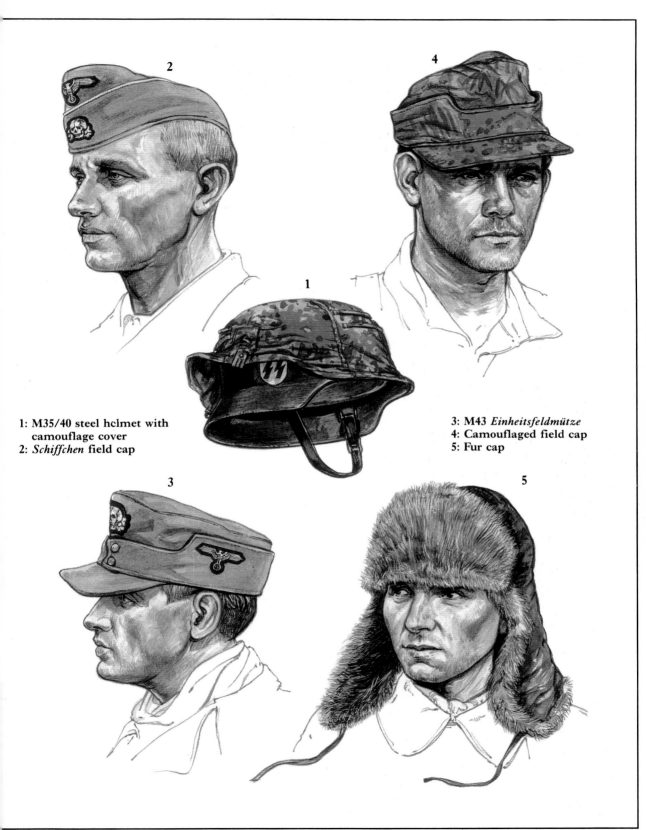

1: M35/40 steel helmet with camouflage cover
2: *Schiffchen* field cap

3: M43 *Einheitsfeldmütze*
4: Camouflaged field cap
5: Fur cap

E

F

1: Early pattern
   camouflage smock
2: Late pattern
   camouflage smock
3: Zeltbahn
4: Army pattern reversible
   winter tunic
5: Waffen-SS pattern
   reversible winter tunic

Putting training into practice, Ardennes 1944

H

1: Obersturmführer,
   Totenkopf Division,
   Russia, summer 1944
2: 9mm Walther P38
   automatic pistol
   (cutaway to show
   internal mechanism)

Kurt 'Panzer' Meyer, became pinned down by heavy and accurate machine-gun fire while trying to force a way through the Klissura Pass. Seeing his men's reluctance to move out of the shelter of the rocks behind which they were crouching, Meyer resorted to the desperate expedient of pulling a pin from a grenade and rolling it towards their feet. 'Never again,' he said later, 'did I witness such a concerted leap forward as at that moment.' The pass was captured and, like Klingenberg, Meyer was awarded the Knights Cross.

Both these examples clearly demonstrate the Waffen-SS determination to win at all costs, as well as their sheer bravado. But there is a far darker side to the character produced by SS psychology and training.

Merville

In May 1940 Theodore Eicke's 'Totenkopf' Division was advancing through France towards Merville. The 4th Company of the 2nd Standarte, commanded by Obersturmführer (Lieutenant) Fritz Knochlein,

The Waffen-SS also included a battalion of Fallschirmjäger (paratroops), the 500th Fallschirmjäger Abteilung. This was formed in September 1943 from members of the SS Bewährungs Abteilung (literally, 'to prove oneself battalion'), a penal unit. The battalion so distinguished itself during a combined parachute and glider operation at Drvar, Bosnia, in 1944, the intention of which was to kill the Yugoslav partisan leader Tito, that Himmler allowed the survivors to put their rank and other insignia back on their completely plain uniforms, and renumbered the battalion 600. (This accounts for some sources saying there were two battalions.) In November 1944 SS-FJR-Abt 600 became part of the SS Jagdverbände, which used Rottweilers in house-to-house searches, but the unit retained its individual identity and ended the war on the eastern front. (Bundesarchiv, Koblenz)

was held up by the determined resistance of an isolated group of about 100 soldiers of the 2nd Royal Norfolk Regiment. Retreating through the little hamlet of Le Paradis, the Norfolks first tried to hold out in a farmhouse but were forced to evacuate it when Knochlein's mortars set it alight. Realising further resistance was futile, the men—who had attempted to find cover in a cowshed—raised a white

flag. They were marched along a lane to a barn outside which two machine-guns had been set up. Lined up in front of it, they were mercilessly gunned down. Incredibly, two men survived the massacre, concealed under the pile of bodies, and when their story emerged at the end of the war Knochlein was brought to trial and hanged. His excuse was that he could not spare men to guard prisoners if the momentum of the advance was to be sustained.

Wormhoudt

The 'Totenkopf' Division was not the only SS unit to be responsible for a massacre during this campaign. At around the same time, the Leibstandarte was closing in on the British Expeditionary Force's perimeter around Dunkirk. Outside the village of Wormhoudt, the car in which 'Sepp' Dietrich was driving came under heavy fire and burst into flames. Dietrich flung himself into a culvert for shelter, rolling in the mud to protect himself from the heat, but it was to be five hours before his men eliminated the resistance and rescued him. Incensed at the

◀ During the raid on Tito's headquarters, the SS Fallschirmjäger were commanded by Otto Skorzeny, who had originally wanted to join the Luftwaffe but transferred to the SS when he found his height precluded him from serving as aircrew. He was responsible for several spectacular exploits, including the rescue of Mussolini after the Italian dictator's downfall in 1943, the kidnapping of Admiral Horthy's son to persuade the Hungarian leader to stay in the war on Germany's side, and commanding Panzer Brigade 150 during the 'Battle of the Bulge', a unit of volunteers dressed in American uniforms and driving American vehicles. Unfortunately, the raid on Drvar failed because Tito escaped. After the war Skorzeny moved to Spain, where he founded the 'Odessa' escape organisation for wanted Nazis on the run, and later he helped President Nasser modernise the Egyptian intelligence service after the Suez débâcle. (Bildarchiv Preussicher Kulturbesitz, Berlin)

Another man who became infamous during the 'Battle of the Bulge' was Joachim Peiper, who was convicted at Nuremberg of responsibility for the massacre of American prisoners at Malmédy. After his release from prison he changed his name and settled in France, but his identity was discovered by former Resistance members and he was murdered in 1975. Here he is seen earlier in the war, during the 1940 campaign in France, as a Hauptsturmführer in the Leibstandarte 'AH'.

thought that their bluff, coarse but beloved commander had been killed, the men of Leibstandarte threw themselves at the defenders of Wormhoudt, some 330 men of the 2nd Royal Warwickshire and Cheshire Regiments and the Royal Artillery. About 80 men were taken prisoner by Haupsturmführer (Captain) Wilhelm Mohnke's company from the regiment's 2nd Battalion, whose own commander had been badly wounded. The men were herded into a barn, whereupon their guards began hurling hand grenades into their midst, shooting down those who tried to escape. Someone finally called a halt to the slaughter, but there were only 15 survivors. The culprit was not identified until 1988, by which time he was an elderly retired businessman.

Oradour-sur-Glane

It was the death of the popular Sturmbannführer (Major) Helmut Kampfe, CO of the 3rd Battalion of the 'Der Führer' Regiment—a predominantly Austrian unit—which provoked one of the worst of all the Waffen-SS massacres. During the evening of 9 June 1944, while the 'Das Reich' Division was *en route* to Normandy, Kampfe set out for his headquarters in his car. When he failed to arrive, men were sent out to look for him. His car was discovered abandoned, but of Kampfe there was no sign, nor was his body ever found. It can safely be assumed that he was ambushed by the *maquis* and killed.

The following morning Kampfe's close friend Otto Dickmann, CO of the 1st Battalion, arrived at regimental headquarters in Limoges in a state of great excitement. Villagers in St Junien had told him that a German officer was being held prisoner by the *maquis* in Oradour-sur-Glane. Dickmann was convinced it must be Kampfe and received permission to investigate. He took the 120 men of his 3rd Company and

drove off, arriving in the sleepy little village early in the afternoon. Dickmann's men raced from house to house, driving their inhabitants into the Champ de Faire. There was no sign of Kampfe or any other German officer. The women and children were herded into the church and the men into barns and garages. Then the shooting began. A total of 648 people died. There were a few lucky survivors, such as three Jewish girls who had managed to stay hidden during the search. When the shooting began, they fled, only to bump straight into an SS private. This man, who has never been identified, gestured for them to run. Dickmann himself never stood trial, being killed in action a few days later.

Perhaps the most infamous of all the Waffen-SS divisional commanders until his death in a plane crash in February 1943 was Theodor Eicke, although he was idolised by the men of his 'Totenkopf' Division to such an extent that a party of volunteers launched an attack through the Russian lines to recover his body. Before assuming command of 'Totenkopf', Eicke had been the first commandant of Dachau concentration camp and later headed the Einsatzgruppen ('special groups', alias extermination squads) in Poland. He was also the man who shot SA leader Ernst Röhm during the 'Night of the Long Knives', June 30 1934. (Bundesarchiv, Koblenz)

What these two stories show is brutality and lack of compassion of the Waffen-SS soldiers and the fierce allegiance they gave to their officers, an allegiance bred from the camaraderie fostered during training and carefully nurtured in the field. Another, less bloodthirsty, example concerns the death of Theodore Eicke. On 26 February 1943, while the 'Totenkopf' Division was engaged near Poltava, Eicke tried unsuccessfully to raise his leading tanks on the radio. Anxious to discover their position, he climbed into his Fieseler Storch with his adjutant and his pilot took off for a reconnaissance. Unfortunately, they strayed over Russian lines and the little aircraft was shot down in flames. Grenadiers in a nearby village attempted to approach the burning wreck but were forced back by heavy machine-gun fire. Word spread rapidly through the division and early the following morning a company of volunteers advanced crouching behind three tanks and two assault guns for cover. They drove the defenders back and recovered the charred bodies. Outside the 'Totenkopf' Division there was little genuine mourning for the man whom his Corps commander in 1940, General Hermann Hoth, had described as 'a butcher and no soldier'.

Almost equally infamous was Brigadeführer Jürgen Stroop (centre), whose men killed an estimated 12,000 Polish Jews during the Warsaw Uprising in April/May 1943. Note the long leather coat worn by the man on Stroop's right, rather more elegant than Theodor Eicke's in the previous photograph, and also the MP 28 carried by the Rottenführer on the right of the photograph. (Bildarchiv Preussicher Kulturbesitz, Berlin)

FAMOUS INDIVIDUALS

Although extremely unpopular except with his own troops, Eicke epitomised several characteristics of the Waffen-SS, particularly brutality. Many other men were of totally different character and showed other characteristics; during the battle for Arnhem in September 1944, for example, the commander of II SS Panzer Korps, Wilhelm Bittrich, ordered his men not only to give captured British paratroopers medical attention, but chocolate and brandy as well. (The ironic fact that these came from captured British supply containers does not detract from the generosity of the deed.)

The 'Hitlerjugend' Division was commanded in Normandy by Fritz Witt until his death during a naval bombardment on June 16 1944. Here Witt is seen a year earlier, as commander of a regimental battlegroup of *the Leibstandarte 'AH' in Russia. He has the collar patches of a Standartenführer and has sacrificed sartorial elegance for warmth with a loose sheepskin jacket. (Bildarchiv Preussicher Kulturbesitz, Berlin)*

Another view of Witt taken at the same time, showing riding breeches tucked into felt boots. Joachim Peiper is on his right wearing what *appears to be a set of dark blue mechanic's overalls on to which a fur collar has been sewn. (Bundesarchiv, Koblenz)*

Broadly speaking, taking their leadership as examples, one can group the men of the Waffen-SS in four categories. Among the 'butchers', alongside Eicke, one could place Friedrich Kruger, last commander of the 6th SS Mountain Division 'Nord', who had earlier terrorised the population of Cracow while commandant there from 1939–44; or Heydrich's former deputy Bruno Streckenbach, who commanded the Latvian 19th SS Grenadier Division with particular brutality. Kurt 'Panzer' Meyer, the miner's son, falls into this category too, and was responsible for a massacre of Canadian prisoners while commanding the 12th SS Panzer Division 'Hitler Jugend' in 1944.

The second category includes professional officers of the old school, such as Paul Hausser, Felix Steiner, Herbert Gille, Wilhelm Bittrich and Georg Keppler. Bittrich, mentioned above, was formerly in the Luftwaffe, but transferred to the Waffen-SS because it offered the prospect of more rapid promotion. Before assuming command of II SS Panzer Korps in 1944 he had earlier led the 8th SS Cavalry and 9th SS Panzer Divisions. He survived the war with the rank of full general. Herbert Gille similarly ended the war with the rank of general, having commanded the 5th SS Panzer Division 'Wiking' during the furious fighting on the Russian Front during 1943–44, and later IV SS Panzer Korps. Felix Steiner, who, as we have seen, fought as an infantryman during the First World War, was director of education at the War Office before transferring to the Waffen-SS in 1935. During the course of the war he actually commanded Army formations on two occasions, III Panzer Korps in 1942 and Eleventh Army during the siege of Berlin in 1945.

Josef 'Sepp' Dietrich really falls into no category.

Uneducated and bluntly outspoken, he had really very little idea of military command and owed his success to his early support of Hitler and the part he played in the Röhm Purge in 1934. After commanding the Leibstandarte since its formation, he became commander of I SS Panzer Korps (succeeding Hausser) from 1943–44, and Sixth SS Panzer Army during the Battle of the Bulge and the last-ditch offensive in Hungary in 1945. Sentenced to 25 years' imprisonment for complicity in war crimes, he was actually released in 1955, still an unrepentant Nazi.

The third class are the foreign volunteers, such as the Romanian Artur Phleps; Woldemaras Veiss, former prime minister of Latvia; and best-known of all, Léon Degrelle, the Belgian fascist leader who commanded the Wallonien Brigade (later Division) throughout the war, particularly distinguishing himself in the rearguard fighting during the breakout from the Cherkassy Pocket.

Finally there are the younger men who, if there is ever glamour in war, gave the Waffen-SS its glamour. These include Theodor Wisch, who assumed command of the Leibstandarte when Dietrich was given I SS Panzer Korps; he was only 37 at the time. Badly wounded, he saw no further action after Normandy. Otto Kumm is another. Only 36 at the end of the war, he commanded the 'Prinz Eugen' Division. Fritz Witt, who was killed by naval gunfire while commanding 'Hitler Jugend', had previously commanded a Leibatandarte battlegroup in Russia. And finally of course there is the hero of Belgrade, Fritz Klingenberg. After the invasion of Russia, he was appointed commander of the officer training school at Bad Tölz, where he himself had learned his trade. In 1945 he was given command of the 17th SS Panzergrenadier Division 'Götz von Berlichingen' and was killed in action only days before the end of the war.

A Waffen-SS officer of completely different character, chivalrous as well as energetic and intelligent, was Wilhelm Bittrich. Like Otto Skorzeny, he had transferred from the Luftwaffe, commanding first the 2nd SS Division 'Das Reich' (1942), then the 8th SS Cavalry Division 'Florian Geyer' (1943), the 9th SS Panzer Division 'Hohenstaufen' (1944) and finally II SS Panzer Korps. His most famous exploit was the defeat of the British and Polish airborne forces at Arnhem in September 1944. (Bundesarchiv, Koblenz)

LOGISTICS

A peculiarity of the Waffen-SS is the struggle they had to acquire modern arms in the early days because the Army insisted they needed everything industry could produce for themselves. As we have seen, this actually worked to their advantage in some respects, such as their acquisition of Bergmann submachine-guns. The Leibstandarte, Hitler's bodyguard, had no problems in obtaining whatever they wanted, because Der Führer insisted on it. The SS-Verfüngungstruppe (which later provided the nucleus for the 'Das Reich' and 'Wiking' Divisions) also managed to get most of what they needed, although there was a shortage of artillery to begin with. But the

The 'Battle of the Bulge', December 1944. Men of the 12th SS Panzer Division 'Hitlerjugend' with American prisoners. The foreground figure carrying the Panzerfaust wears coarse twill camouflage trousers as well as smock, while other men have the leather U-boat jackets which were almost unique to this formation. (Bildarchiv Preussicher Kulturhesitz, Berlin)

Army was opposed to helping Eicke in any way, and only grudgingly, under pressure from Hitler, agreed to accept a few of his men for specialist training, at the signals school in Halle, for example. But for weapons and equipment Eicke had to scour his own concentration camp stores and other SS depots, even resorting to 'borrowing' a couple of old howitzers used for training purposes at Bad Tölz.

As 1939 drew to a close, thanks to Himmler's constant entreaties to Hitler, Eicke's 'Totenkopf' Division gradually began to come together. Much of his equipment was Czech, but there was nothing wrong in this because the Czech arms industry was one of the finest in the world—and, in fact, during the 1940 campaign, roughly a quarter of the Army's tanks were also Czech. What annoyed Eicke was the fact that when Himmler managed to acquire a dozen Skoda 15 cm artillery pieces, they went to the Verfüngungstruppe instead of the 'Totenkopf'.

Nevertheless, the eminent American historian George H. Stein (see bibliography) makes the following interesting comment. On 4 April 1940 the commander of the Second Army, General Freiherr

Maximilian von Weichs, paid his first visit to the new formation which had been placed under his command:

'In their opening conversation with Eicke, Weichs and his staff revealed their ignorance ... They were under the impression that the "Toten-kopf" Division was organised and equipped like a Czech foot division, and were very much surprised to discover it was really a modern, motorised infantry division. At a time when only seven of the Army's 139 infantry divisions were motorised, this was indeed a command to be proud of. Weichs' inspection of the troops left him visibly impressed, and he completed his visit in a frame of mind far different from that in which he had arrived.' (Weichs was not the only high-ranking Army officer to be impressed by the 'Toten-kopf'. Later in the war, Germany's greatest general, Field Marshal Erich von Manstein, came to consider it the finest unit under his command.)

After the Waffen-SS had proved itself in the 1940 campaign and Hitler authorised further expansion,

army reluctance to help gradually receded. Then, as Hitler came to place increasing reliance on the fighting ability and loyalty of his Waffen-SS formations, they actually began to receive priority in the allocation of new equipment. This led to the popular but totally untrue myth that the reason for the Waffen-SS's success was because it was better equipped than the Army. It was not, although it did de-centralise its weapons allocation, which could have fostered that impression, because each squad of eight men had at least one machine-gun, so a platoon of three squads had a minimum of three plus at least one mortar. Similarly, of the three or four platoons in a company, one would be a support platoon equipped entirely with machine-guns and mortars, in line with the Waffen-SS's emphasis on maximum firepower to achieve results. In the Army, although the basic organisation was the same, machine-guns were only allocated at platoon rather than squad level.

The Waffen-SS could never acquire enough automatic weapons from official sources for its satisfaction, so the bounty of captured weapons following the mass encirclement battles during the initial phases of the Russian campaign was welcomed with open arms. Kar 98s were thrown away in favour of Tokarev self-loading rifles, PPD and PPSh

Arnhem. A StuG III assault gun rumbles past wounded British paras. The SS soldier with his back to the camera is wearing a 1943 pattern drill jacket and 1944 pattern herringbone trousers. (Bundesarchiv, Koblenz)

submachine-guns and Degtyarev light machine-guns, all adding to the Waffen-SS's already formidable firepower. These weapons proved their value in particular during the vicious street fighting which characterised such a large part of the Russian campaign.

The German manufacturing and supply organisation was, by and large, remarkably efficient, but it became strained beyond its limits in Russia. During the first winter of 1941–42, for example, there was never enough warm clothing because the high command had incorrectly predicted the campaign would be over in six weeks. As a result, the men had to acquire whatever they could, the result being that virtually all pretence at uniform disappeared as they wrapped themselves in 'commandeered' fur and sheepskin coats and hats.

The basis of the German supply organisation was the railway system, although petrol was brought forward in convoys of tanker trucks. Everything else—food, ammunition, medical supplies, etc—was transported to railheads and thence to depots from which individual battalions and companies collected their requirements in their own trucks. Unfortunately, this system frequently broke down, either because of the weather or because of partisan attacks on the railway lines and convoy routes. The Luftwaffe helped as much as possible, but lacked enough aircraft with sufficient payload to be of more than marginal help, especially since the weather all too often prevented flying at all. This meant that the supply administrators had to put the emphasis on ammunition, with everything else given second priority, so for food the men all too frequently had to forage for themselves as so many armies have had to throughout history.

COLLECTING

Where SS items are concerned, the answer here more than in any other sphere of military memorabilia is 'caveat emptor'. Such has been the profusion of Third Reich fakes and replicas that even the most astute dealers are sometimes fooled, while others are undeniably rogues. Nor is price any realistic guide to actual value. It is best to deal through one of the reputable auction houses, such as Sothebys,

A slightly different style of tropical jacket was issued to men serving in southern Russia, such as this Hauptscharführer of the 'Wiking' Division, and to members of the Sturmbrigade (later 16th SS Panzergrenadier Division) *'Reichsführer-SS' when they were stationed on Corsica in 1943. This tunic incorporated a 'sahariana'-style yoke and photographic evidence suggests collar patches were rarely worn. (Bundesarchiv, Koblenz)*

Christies, Wallis and Wallis or Phillips, who hold regular sales of arms, armour and medals throughout the year and who offer money-back guarantees if an item turns out to be a fake. Specialist magazines such as *Military Illustrated* regularly carry advertisements from dealers specialising in Third Reich memorabilia, most of whom can supply catalogues of items currently available and who are well aware of the problem of fakes. Beware especially of militaria flea markets; unless you really know the subject, you could end up paying a substantial price for pure junk. Beware especially of personalised items such as daggers, death's head rings and medal citations, which are easily forged with modern laser copiers. Less valuable (because more common) items such as the Wehrpass and Soldbuch are most likely to be genuine, but examine any medal awards in them carefully because it is easy for the unscrupulous to add an award in order to increase the document's value. Two excellent guides are Chris Ailsby's *Combat Medals of the Third Reich* (Patrick Stephens Ltd) and Robin Lumsden's *The Black Corps: A collector's guide to the History and Regalia of the SS* (Ian Allan Ltd).

MUSEUMS AND COLLECTIONS

There is not, so far as I am aware, any museum specialising in Waffen-SS memorabilia, but the following list includes the best of what can be seen outside private collections.

Imperial War Museum, Lambeth, London, England.
Imperial War Museum, Land Warfare Hall, Duxford, Cambs, England.

Bovington Tank Museum, near Wool, Dorset, England.
Wehrtechnische Studiensammlung, BWB, Koblenz, Germany.
Auto und Technik Museum, Sinsheim, near Heidelberg, Germany.
Panzermuseum, Munster, Germany.
Aberdeen Proving Ground, Maryland, USA.
Patton Armor Museum, Fort Knox, Kentucky, USA.
Saumur Armour Museum, Loire Valley, France.
Musée Memorial, Bayeux, France.
Diekirch Historical Museum, Diekirch, Luxembourg.
Panzermuseum, Thun, Switzerland.

THE PLATES

A1: Hauptsturmführer (Captain) of the Leibstandarte 'Adolf Hitler', Röhm Purge, 30 June 1934

Typifying the Hollywood stereotype of an SS officer, this captain clasping a smoking 9 mm P08 Luger is dressed in the all-black uniform which would later be reserved for ceremonial duties, and was shared (with different insignia) by members of the Allgemeine or General SS. For headgear he wears the smart service dress cap (Tellermütze) with SS-pattern eagle and the Totenkopf device which was shared with personnel of the army Panzertruppen. (This has been a favoured cavalry symbol in many nations for hundreds of years, but the Waffen-SS made it peculiarly their own, symbolising their willingness to die for their cause.) His collar patches bear the SS Sigrunen on the right and the three pips plus two bars of his rank on the left. His shoulder boards have the distinctive 'LAH' monogram in silver and he wears a Party armband on his left sleeve above the black and silver regimental cuff title.

A2: 9 mm Luger P08 automatic pistol

This illustrates the standard version with 102 mm

A machine-gunner of the 'Totenkopf' Division chats to a Hungarian soldier in Budapest, 1945. The tubes slung across his back contain spare barrels for his MG 34 or '42. Behind the men is a Tiger II of schwere Panzer Abteilung 503, an army formation. (Bundesarchiv, Koblenz)

barrel and is drawn in cutaway form to show the spring-loaded toggle lock system and method of ammunition feed from the eight-round spring clip magazine.

B1: 9 mm Schmeisser (Haenel) MP28 submachine-gun

Like the Erma and Bergmann, this weapon with its side-loading magazine and wooden stock was preferred by the Waffen-SS rather than the more modern MP38 and 40. (See text for description.)

B2: 9 mm Bergmann MP 34/35 submachine-gun

Manufacture of this Danish weapon was taken over by Walther and Junker after 1940, the entire production—which only totalled 40,000—going to the Waffen-SS. It was an extremely popular weapon, but surviving examples in good condition are rare. (See text for additional details.)

B3: 9 mm MP38 and 40 submachine-gun

Manufactured by Erfurter Maschinenfabrik, Haenel and Suhl, this was the most common German submachine-gun of the war. It was made in several variants, including the so-called MP 40/II, which allowed two 32-round magazines to be held in the housing and slid across to save time reloading, but it was prone to jamming and weighed too much to be comfortable. (See text for additional details.)

B4: Leather and canvas MP38/MP40 magazine packs

These could also hold the magazines for the MP 28, '35 and MPE and were worn on the waistbelt, a normal arrangement being three pouches either side of the buckle.

B5: 7.92 mm MP43 assault rifle

Developed from the Haenel MKb 42 and first issued to the troops in time for the battle of Kursk in July 1943, this weapon was manufactured by Haenel, Erfurter Maschinenfabrik and Mauser. See text for further details. Later in the war, Hitler relented in his decision about the nomenclature for this class of weapon and it became known as the StG 44 (Sturmgewehr 44, or Assault rifle model 44). Early versions had a clamp-on grenade launcher but later ones a screw fitting. Additionally, an unusual 'optional extra' was a curved barrel adaptor (*Krummlauf*) with a mirror sight which enabled the weapon to be fired around corners. This reduced muzzle velocity and

or five warheads could be strapped around one central one to multiply the blast effect, which was particularly useful in attacking enemy trenches or pillboxes.

B9: 7.9 mm MG42 machine-gun

A general-purpose weapon which could be used as a sustained fire weapon mounted on a tripod, giving a range of over 3,000 m, or as here on a bipod as a light machine-gun. Barrel heating was a major problem, so crews always carried spares which could quickly be exchanged. In the LMG role, it was difficult to control properly, but the high rate of fire more than made up for this. Despite being of 'inferior' manufacturing quality to the MG 34, it needed less cleaning and was better able to stand up to rough treatment.

C1: Riflemen's 'Y' straps with 'D' rings and belt

Made of black or brown leather with mild steel fastenings, this clipped to the back of the waistbelt and passed over the shoulders to be fastened suspender-style at the front. All of an infantryman's standard kit was fastened to this and the waistbelt. The front straps were 4 cm wide tapering towards the 'D' ring and the waist while the single back strap was 2.5 cm wide. A lightweight web yoke could be attached to carry the assault pack in combat, but full equipment included *Zeltbahn*, greatcoat and blanket.

C2a: NCO and other ranks' belt buckle
2b: Officer's belt buckle

The rectangular plate on the left is for NCOs and other ranks, the circular clasp and locket one on the right for officers. Both bear the Waffen-SS motto 'Mein Ehre heist Treue' (Loyalty is my Honour or My Honour is Loyalty). Both were stamped in white metal.

C3: M1931 field flask and drinking cup

Made of aluminium or mild steel, with aluminium or Bakelite cups, and with or without a felt or wood insulation covering, these oval canteens were kidney-

range but, because it was principally intended for use in street fighting, that factor did not matter overmuch. Needless to say, the *Krummlauf* was not a great success under operational conditions.

B6: Leather and canvas MP43 magazine pouches

B7: M1939 Eiergranate

The standard German 'egg grenade' weighed 0.34 kg, could be thrown to about 45 m and had a blast radius of some 13 m. Later in the war, and largely at Waffen-SS insistence, segmented fragmentation sleeves were sometimes attached to increase its effectiveness.

B8: M1924 Stielhandgranate

The common 'stick grenade', so called because of its handle, was heavier than the egg grenade (0.59 kg) so could not be thrown so far, but had two advantages. A number could be tucked into the belt ready for instant use, rather than carried in a satchel; and four

shaped in cross section to hang snugly and held 0.8 litre of water.

C4: Small entrenching tool with 'closed-back' carrier

A simple spade with a square steel blade and short wood handle. The blade's edge was sometimes sharpened so that it could double as an improvised close-quarter weapon.

▼ Anti-tank guns were, in some respects, more important than tanks themselves during the Second World War. They were not only cheaper to manufacture but much more easily concealed, and a well-trained crew could inflict hideous casualties on enemy armour. The men serving this 7.5 cm Pak 40 have already racked up 23 'kills'. (Christopher Ailsby Historical Archives)

▶ One of the most successful anti-tank gunners of the war was Sturmann Remy Schrÿnen, a Belgian member of the 27th SS Freiwilligen Division 'Langemarck', seen here accompanied by Untersturmführer Koslovsky on the occasion of his being awarded the Knights Cross for single-handedly knocking out seven Soviet tanks even though wounded at the time. (Christopher Ailsby Historical Archives)

Obersturmführer Erwin Meierdress, commander of an assault gun battery in the 'Totenkopf' Division, photographed on the hospital steps while recovering from the wounds received during an engagement in Russia which won him the Knights Cross on March 13 1942. He wears the standard SS pattern double-breasted field grey jacket for SPG personnel. Meierdress was killed in action in April 1945. (Bundesarchiv, Koblenz)

C5: S84/98 bayonet and dismounted sidearm carrier

There were several styles of bayonet, none of them unique to the Waffen-SS, so if you are a collector and come across a dress version with the SS runes set in a small circle on the obverse of the hilt (the side which fits into the palm of the hand) you should make very sure it is not a fake. If the SS runes are on the other side of the hilt, it is definitely a fake. The example illustrated is the most common 84/98 pattern with straight crossguard; the 98/04 pattern was similar but had curved quillons, while bayonets manufactured during the Third Reich period were shorter-bladed—248 mm compared with 252–300 mm on these early First World War pattern bayonets. Some

had plain blades while others were Parkerized (ie, treated with phosphoric acid then blackened by burning off an oil coating, to make them less reflective in bright sunlight or at night). The scabbard was of leather and could be clipped to the waistbelt or on the entrenching tool.

C6: 1936 Pattern SS dagger

The second and most common pattern dagger which was conferred on all personnel of Scharführer (Sergeant) rank and higher, and from 30 January 1936 available for purchase by men of any rank who had served in the SS for a minimum of three years. (The earlier 1933 pattern dagger is a far more rare and therefore expensive collector's item. It can be distinguished by the maker's name and mark as well as the word SOLINGEN on the blade close to the hilt, together with the Roman numerals I, II or III for the issuing authority—Munich, Dresden or Berlin respectively—and will usually have the original owner's name engraved on the obverse.) Both pattern daggers had the motto 'Mein Ehre heist Treue' on the obverse of the blade, in one of three Gothic lettering styles. The hilt was of blackened wood with steel crossguard and pommel in the same shape as the traditional German hunting knife. It incorporated a small silver eagle clutching a swastika in a wreath in the centre of the obverse and the SS runes in a small circle close to the pommel on the same side. The blued metal scabbard was attached to the waistbelt by leather straps (33 pattern) or metal links (36 pattern), the latter featuring alternating death's heads and SS runes. Honour daggers, awarded for meritorious conduct, were much more elaborate with the crossguard and pommel decorated with acorns and oak-leaves and silver-plated. Although basically a mark of distinction, the SS dagger was a useful combat tool as well.

C7: M1938 gasmask case

Made of fluted mild steel or aluminium painted field grey, the respirator container was usually slung around the neck on a double canvas loop. In the field, it was frequently used to carry cigarettes to keep them dry.

C8: M1931 cook pot

Lightweight aluminium container painted field grey

with carrying handle folded underneath. The lid served as a plate. The paint on the mess tin and gasmask container soon chipped.

C9: M1911 cartridge pouches

Usually made of leather (or, later, imitation leather), these were normally carried in threes either side of the belt buckle. Each pouch carried a five-round clip of 7.92 mm bullets.

D1: Unterscharführer (Sergeant) of the 1st SS-VT Standarte 'Deutschland', France, June 1940

Holding his early-pattern sidecap with triangular embroidered SS eagle on its left side while he wipes sweat from his face, this NCO is dressed in the standard field grey tunic and trousers which became regulation wear for the Waffen-SS after 1937, with dark green collar and slanting slash pockets in the sides of the skirts. His right collar patch bears the Sigrunen together with the number '1', denoting his regiment (only 'Deutschland', 'Germania' and 'Der Führer' were so numbered) while that on the left

bears the single pip of his rank. Note the regimental 'D' monogram on his shoulder boards and cuff title on his left sleeve below the SS arm eagle. He wears standard thigh-length iron-nailed leather marching boots and carries a 7.92 mm Kar 98k rifle, while on the front of his belt is the wooden holster-stock for a 9 mm C 96 Mauser automatic pistol, held on by brown leather straps, with a screwdriver attached on its side.

D2: 9 mm C 96 Mauser automatic pistol

Again shown in cutaway, this illustrates the standard version with ten-round magazine, loaded loose from the top. It will be readily apparent where the weapon acquired its nickname 'broomhandle Mauser', this uncomfortable grip being the pistol's worst feature. A selector switch enabled it to be fired single-shot or fully automatic.

E1: M35/40 helmet and camouflage cover
The standard field grey steel helmet with crimped edge being worn with a summer-pattern camouflage cover. The SS decal replaced the army eagle on the right-hand side of the helmet. Helmet covers were produced in the same patterns as the smocks and varied only in their fastening detail. Some later war patterns, as here, had loops into which foliage could be tucked.

E2: Schiffchen *field cap*
Replacing the earlier pattern side cap seen in Plate B1, this had a scalloped brim and national eagle sewn at the front above the Totenkopf device. The soutache is white, the infantry colour.

E3: M43 Einheitsfeldmütze
Largely replacing the earlier side cap, certainly from 1943 onwards, this more practical form of headgear was based on the mountain trooper's cap (*Bergmütze*) which had a shorter visor. It existed in several variations with one or two frontal buttons, not all of them authorised, due to wartime exigencies, but this is one of the most common. The national eagle could be sewn above the frontal Totenkopf or on the left-hand side.

E4: Camouflaged field cap
This was a lightweight version of the Einheitsfeld-mütze in camouflage material and usually lacking both buttons and insignia, although private-purchase caps with both do exist.

Hated almost as much as flamethrowers were the SS Feldgendarmerie (field police), who were nicknamed 'chained dogs' because of their distinctive gorgets. Note also cuff title. This Scharführer appears to be showing Russian prisoners photographs of – presumably – wanted men. (Bundesarchiv, Koblenz)

E5: Fur cap

Produced to help counter the bitter cold of the Russian winters, this was a fur-lined felt cap with deep ear flaps and a chin string which could be used to tie the flaps at the crown when the weather was warmer. It was not issued with any insignia although men often sewed their own on.

F1: Early pattern camouflage smock

This example shows the screen-printed smock first worn in Poland and the invasion of the west. The summer pattern is outside but the autumn pattern can be seen inside the neck opening. Features to note are the low elasticated waist, elasticated cuffs, and the two slits in the chest to enable the wearer to reach the pockets of his tunic underneath. In practice, when worn with the standard 'Y' strap webbing, this proved impossible, so the vents were omitted on later pattern smocks. These original smocks, of rayon/cotton duck cloth, were printed by a lengthy process necessitating up to six screens, and it could take several days (including waterproofing, which could not be done until the dyes were dry) to produce a single batch. Later smocks were mainly machine-printed to save time.

F2: Late pattern camouflage smock

Several differences are immediately apparent. The chest vents have gone, to be replaced by patch pockets on the lower skirt. Buttons replace drawstrings a the neck and, although the wrists and waist remain elasticated, the latter is higher and more comfortable. Additionally, thin strips of material are sown on the upper part of the garment so that leaves and twigs can be inserted for additional camouflage. This garment shows the autumn pattern outside, summer inside.

F3: Zeltbahn

This triangular piece of kit was extremely useful, being small and light enough to be carried as part of the assault equipment and serving as a poncho, windbreak or part of a tent. Because of the loopholes along each edge, two or more could be laced together, supported by an upturned rifle or tree branch; but it could be carried as a small roll or worn either loose or wrapped around the legs and upper arms. Most Zeltbahns were either plain field grey or in army pattern camouflage, but towards the end of the war examples in SS camouflage did appear.

F4: Army pattern reversible winter tunic

This shows a front view of the standard grey/white reversible winter anorak with hood shared by both the army and the Waffen-SS, although to begin with (1942) the SS received priority in its allocation. It was lined with blanket material for warmth and, like the smock, was truly reversible. It also had a storm flap at the throat. Earlier in the war, the troops had had to make do with improvised snow camouflage smocks of thin white sheeting which they tied over their greatcoats. The new anorak assisted mobility enormously as well as helping to keep the men warm.

F5: Waffen-SS pattern reversible winter tunic

Inevitably, the Waffen-SS were not slow in producing their own pattern of reversible winter clothing with the non-white side in autumnal camouflage. This shows the rear view. Because almost all Waffen-SS clothing was manufactured in concentration camps, the tailoring was erratic and often shoddy, although this was more often due to the simple effects of deprivation and hunger than to deliberate sabotage.

G: Panzerfaust training

Here a young 17-year-old grenadier from the 12th SS Panzer Division 'Hitlerjugend' is being shown how to use the *Panzerfaust* by a grizzled Unterscharführer. Most of the 'Hitlerjugend' officers were drawn from the Leibstandarte, and this sergeant proudly retains the cuff title of his parent formation. The 'rookie' wears the 1944 pattern *Feldbluse*, a coarse garment resembling the British BD blouse made from *Zeltbahn* material. It was not reversible. His helmet is plain anodised steel with no decals, as was common towards the end of the war. The sergeant-instructor is from an assault gun unit and wears the SS-pattern self-propelled gun crew trousers and double-breasted blouse with red waffenfarbe. His right sleeve carries three tank destruction badges, while on the left front of his tunic are a tank assault badge and ribbon of the Iron Cross. On his head is a field grey *Einheitsfeldmütze* with Totenkopf on the peak and national eagle on the left-hand side. The *Panzerfaust* was extremely easy to operate, even by 'raw' troops, although it required guts. (See text for further details.)

In jovial mood at the start of the French campaign in May 1940 – even Himmler wears a rare smile – Obergruppenführer 'Sepp' Dietrich radiates confidence in the ability of the Leibstandarte 'AH', a confidence which was not misplaced. (Bildarchiv Preussicher Kulturhesitz, Berlin)

H: Putting training into practice, Ardennes 1944

Now muffled in reversible white winter parka and overtrousers with no insignia, our 'Hitlerjugend' recruit has survived the Normandy battles to take part in Hitler's last great gamble in the west. He is now equipped with a second pattern *Panzerschreck* with shield. (For details, see text.) His loader, slapping his shoulder to indicate the weapon is loaded, has a pair of anti-tank Tellermines. These came in a variety of sizes from 254 to 324 mm in diameter and 6 to 9.75 kg in weight, and could penetrate up to 24 mm of armour plate, which was sufficient to pierce the relatively thin undersides of any tank or knock off a roadwheel and damage several track links.

I1: Obersturmführer (Lieutenant) of the 'Totenkopf' Division, Russia, summer 1944

Illustrated during the long 'advance to the rear' in which the Waffen-SS divisions acted as a mobile fire brigade to stem the Soviet advance, this war-weary officer still shows pride in his bearing even though his face betrays exhaustion. He wears the 'old style' officer's cap without stiffening, the 1943-pattern tailored camouflage jacket and 1944-pattern trousers, a typical field combination given the usual supply vagaries. He also wears the ankle boots with canvas gaiters which by this time had more or less superseded the thigh-length marching boots due to considerations of comfort and endurance. Rank and unit insignia are missing, quite common by this stage of the war, but he has sewn an SS eagle on his sleeve in contradiction of regulations—as in many other such matters, the troops in the field were a law unto themselves. For weaponry, he carries a 9 mm Erma MPE submachine-gun and has a holstered Walther P38 on his belt. The Vollmer-designed MPE with its distinctive fore-grip and double trigger (the latter also being a feature of the MP 34/35) was another of those pre-war designs shunned by the army but lapped up by the Waffen-SS because of its superior construction and reliability, as well as the fact that its 25- or 32-round magazine was inserted from the side instead of beneath. Performance was similar to that of the MP28 or MP34/35 (see text).

I2: 9 mm P38 Walther automatic pistol

The standard German sidearm from 1940, the P38 incorporated several design improvements over the Luger, including the better shaped grip and trigger and a 'safety pin' showing when there was a round in the breech. It was (and is) such a good weapon that production was resumed for the post-war Bundeswehr in 1957.

Bibliography

So many books have been published on the subject of the SS that it is only possible to make a selection of recommended titles. A large number exist additionally in the German language, specifically very detailed multi-volume unit histories, usually with very good photographs but also extremely expensive. These can be sought out through any specialist military bookshop who advertises in military magazines.

Bender, R. J., and Taylor, H. P.: *Uniforms, Organization and History of the Waffen-SS* (4 vols), Bender-Taylor Publishing, 1969–75. Superb highly illustrated study.

Butler, Rupert: *The Black Angels*, Hamlyn, 1978. A well-written, fastmoving, general introduction.

Graber, G. S.: *History of the SS*, Robert Hale, 1978. Deals with the SS as a whole, but good.

Hohne, Heinz: *The Order of the Death's Head*, Martin Secker & Warburg, 1969. Despite its age, still the best general introduction to the SS as a whole.

Keegan, John: *Waffen-SS: The Asphalt Soldiers*, Ballantine, 1970. One of that lovely Ballantine series, long out of print, well worth buying if you can find a copy.

Mollo, Andrew: *Uniforms of the SS* (7 vols, of which Vol 6 is specifically devoted to the Waffen-SS), Windrow & Greene, 1991–93. Alongside the Bender-Taylor books, the most important of all for uniform and insignia detail.

Quarrie, Bruce: *Lightning Death*, Patrick Stephens, 1991. General introduction containing information unknown to earlier authors such as Butler or Keegan but otherwise telling much the same story.

Quarrie, Bruce: *Hitler's Samurai*, Patrick Stephens, 1984. Explores the theory that the SS philosophy was actually based on that of the medieval samurai.

Quarrie, Bruce: *Hitler's Teutonic Knights*, Patrick Stephens, 1986. Illustrated unit histories of the seven SS Panzer divisions.

Reitlinger, Gerald: *The SS: Alibi of a Nation*, Heinemann, 1956. The classic study, very scholarly, lacking the detail of more modern research but the first book to examine the moral issue of making the SS responsible for all the ills of Nazi Germany.

Stein, George H.: *The Waffen-SS: Hitler's Elite Guard at War*, Cornell University Press, 1966. The second classic study and still very well worth reading.

Steven, Andrew, and Amodio, Peter: *Waffen-SS Uniforms in Colour Photographs*, Windrow & Greene, 1990. One of a new range of excellent reference books illustrating models dressed in authentic uniforms and kit.

Wenn Alle Bruder Schweigen, Munin Verlag, 1973. Dual-language text, large format, hundreds of photos; the Waffen-SS's own effort to portray themselves as all 'jolly good chaps'.

Windrow, Martin: *The Waffen-SS*, Osprey, 1982. Revised edition of a classic work in the 'Men-at-Arms' series.

Notes sur les planches en couleur

A1 Cet 'Hauptsturmführeris' est armé d'un Luger Po8 9mm et est habillé d'un uniforme noir-uni qui sera utilisé plus tard seulement comme tenue de cérémonie. Il porte la casquette de service (Tellermütze) avec l'aigle des SS et l'insigne tête de mort. Sur les pièces du col on voit les runes des SS sur la droite et les insignes de rang à la gauche. A2 Version régulière du pistolet automatique Luger Po8 avec un canon de 102mm. Le schéma écorché illustre le levier articulé à ressort et la méthode de chargement à ressort à huit coups.

B1 Mitraillette MP28 Schmeisser 9mm (Haenel). B2 Mitraillette MP 34/35 Bergmann 9mm. B3 Mitraillettes MP38 et 40 9mm. B4 Etuis en cuir et en toile pour la MP40. B5 Fusil d'assault MP43 7.92mm. B6 Etuis en cuir et en toile pour la MP43. B7 Grenade ovoïde M1939. B8 Grenade à manche. B9 Mitraillette 7.92mm MG42.

C1 Equipment d'ordonnance à lanières (avec anneau en forme 'D' et lanière en forme 'Y'). Fabriquées en cuir marron ou noir avec des attaches en acier à l'arrière de la ceinture, les lanières passent par dessus les épaules pour s'attacher au devant. Les lanières au devant mesurent 4cm de large et passent dans l'anneau 'D' et puis à la taille, tandis que la lanière unique au dos mesure 2.5cm de largeur. C2 La plaque rectangulaire à la gauche est réservée au sous officier ainsi qu'aux autres rangs. Mais le fermoir circulaire et la boucle à gauche sont pour les officiers. Les deux articles sont poinçonnés sur de métal blanc. C3 Fabriqués en aluminium ou en acier mou. Certains sont isolés avec du feutre ou du bois. En forme de haricot, ils contiennent 0.8 litres d'eau. C4 L'outil à retranchement avec le premier modèle d'emballage en cuir. C5 La baïonnette à motif 84/98 à ergot droit. Le fourreau est fabriqué en cuir et s'attache à la ceinture ou à l'outil de retranchement. C6 Poignard datant de 1936 à manche en bois noirci. L'ergot et le pommeau sont en acier. Le fourreau de métal

Farbtafeln

A1 Dieser Hauptsturmführer trägt eine 9mm Luger Po8 und die Uniform ganz in Schwarz, die später nur für Paradezwecke getragen wurde. Er trägt die Tellermütze mit dem SS-Adler und Totenkopfabzeichen. Am Kragen hat er die SS-Runen rechts und dazs Rangabzeichen links. A2 Die Standard-Version der automatischen Pistole Luger Po8 mit 102mm-Lauf. Dile Waffe ist in Schnittdarstellung gezeichnet, um das fedetgelaugte Kniehebelsperrsystem ebenzo zu zeigen wie den Patronentransport vom achtschüssigen Federmagazin.

B1 9mm-Maschinenpistole Schmeißer (Haenel) MP28. *B2* 9mm-Maschinenpistole Bergmann MP34/35. B3 9mm-Maschinenpistolen MP38 und 40. B4 Leder-und Segeltuchtaschen für MP40. B5 7,92mm-Gewehr MP43. B6 Leder-und Segeltuchtaschen für MP43. B7 Eierhandgranaten M1939. B8 Stielhandgranate. B9 7,92mm-Maschinengewehr MG42.

C1 D-Ring-, Y-Reimengurten aus braunem oder schwarzen Leder mit Weichstahlschlüsseln, angebracht hinten am Gürtel und über die Schulter nach vorn geführt und dort befestigt. Die vorderen Riemen waren 4cm breit und schmäler zulaufend gegen den D-Ring und die Taille zu; der einteilige Rückenriemen war 2,5cm breit. C2 Die rechteckige Platte links ist für Unterroffiziere und ähnliche Ränge bestimmt, die runde Schließe und die Schnalle rechts für Offiziere. Beide waren aus Weißmetall gestanzt. C3 Feldflaschen aus Aluminium oder Weichstahl, mit Aluminium- oder Bakelitbechern. Manche hatten Filz- oder Holzüberzug; sie waren im Querschnitt nierenförmig und faßten 0,8 Liter Wasser. C4 Faltbares Grabewerkzeug mit Holzgriff, ursprünglich in Lederbehälter. C5 Ein Bajonett Muster 84/98 mit geradem Stichblatt. Die Lederscheide konnte am Gürtel oder am Grabewerkzeug befestigt werden. C6 SS-Dolch von 1936 mit Knauf aus geschwärztem Holz, Stahl-Stichblatt und Quaste. Die Scheide aus blauem Metall

bleuté est attaché à la ceinture par des anneaux méttaliques. C7 Les récipients pour porter les masques à gaz sont en acier cannelé ou en aluminium et sont peints en gris réglementaire. C8 Les gamelles légères ont la poignée sur le dessous. On utilise le couvercle comme assiette. C9 Les étuis à munitions Kar 98 en aluminium sont fabriqués d'habitide en cuir ou plus tard pendant la guerre, en imitation cuir. Chaque étui contient deux chargeurs avec cinq cartouches de 7.92mm.

D1 Ce sergent est habillé avec la tunique et le pantalon gris devenus tenue régulière pou les Waffen-SS après 1937. Il porte les bottes de marche d'ordonnance et un fusil Kar 98k 7.92mm. A sa ceinture on voit l'étui en bois pour un pistolet automatique Mauser C96 9mm. D2 Le schéma du Mauser C96 illustre le chargeur à dix coups, chargé par le haut. Un bouton sélecteur permet le tirage à simple coup ou automatique.

E1 Le casque régulier en acier gris a un bord irrégulier et est couvert du motif de camouflage d'été. Le motif des SS remplace l'aigle de l'armée sur le côté droit du casque. E2 Le Feldmûtze remplace l'ancienne casquette et porte la bordure à festons. E3 A partir de 1943, le Einheitsfeldmûtze remplace de manière générale la casquette de côte. Cette casquette a pour origine la casquette du soldat de montagne et elle existe en plusiers modèles. Celle-ci avec les deux boutons est la plus commune. On peut coudre l'aigle sur le côté gauche ou devant, au dessus de l'insigne tête de mort. E4 Version légère de la casquette réglementaire avec tissu de camouflage. E5 Casquette doublée de fourrure avec des pièces pour protéger les oreilles contre le grand froid des hivers en Russie.

F1 On voit ici une des premières blouses imprimées. On la porte en Pologne et pendant l'invasion de l'ouest. On voit ici la version d'été mais celle de l'automne est visible à l'ouverture du col. F2 Version plus récente de la blouse de camouflage. Les pièces à la poitrine sont remplacées par des poches sur la jupe. On remplace les boutons par des ficelles de fermeture au niveau du col. La taille est plus haute que sur la version précédente. Sur l'extérieur de la blouse on voit le camouflage d'automne, et à l'intérieur le camouflage d'été. F3 La plupart des 'Zaltbahns' sont gris unis ou à motif de camouflage d'ordonnance, mais à la fin de la guerre on en voit quelques uns qui portent le motif de camouflage des SS. F4 L'anorak d'ordonnance réversible blue-blanc pour l'hiver avec une capuche est utilisé par l'armée ainsi que les Waffen SS. Il est doublé avec une tissu épais comme une couverture pour garder la chaleur. Une pièce spéciale est attachée au niveau de la gorge. F5 L'arrière de la tunique d'hiver réversible.

G Un sergent apprend à ce jeune grenadier de la 12ème division SS Panzer 'Hitlerjugend' à utiliser le 'Panzerfaust'.

H L'équipe à la recherche de tanks dans les Ardennes pendant la dernière offensive de l'ouest. Ils sont équipés du second modèle du 'Panzerschreck' avec une paire de 'Tellermines'. Le chargeur frappe l'épaule de son grenadier qui opère le 'Panzerschreck' pour lui indiquer que c'est désormais armé.

I1 Ce lieutenant porte la casquette d'officer de l'ancien style, la veste de camouflage datant de 1943 et le pantalon de 1944. Il porte aussi les bottes au niveau des chevilles avec des guêtres en toile qui ont quasiment remplacé les grandes bottes de marche à hauteur des cuisses. Il manque les insignes de range et d'unité mais on a cousu l'insigne des SS avec l'aigle sur la manche. Il porte une mitraillette Erma MPE 9mm et un Walther P38 9mm avec étui. I2 L'arme régulière de 1940 est le Walther P39 9mm. Cette arme a subi beaucoup d'améliorations, en comparaison avec le Luger. Le Walther a une prise et une gâchette qui sont plus pratiques et un cran de sécurité pour rapeller qu'il y a un coup dans la culasse.

war durch Metallglieder am Gürtel befestigt. C7 Gasmaskenbehälter aus gerieftem Weichstahl oder Aluminium, und feldgrau gestrichen. C8 Das leichte Kochgeschirr war aus Aluminium, mit darunter gefaltetem Handgriff. Der Deckel diente als Teller. C9 Munitionstaschen Kar 98 bestanden meist aus Leder, später aus Lederimitation. Jede Tasche enthielt zwei fünfschüssige Munitionsstreifen Kaliber 7,92mm.

D1 Dieser Gefreite trägt die normale feldgraue Bluse und Hose, die nach 1937 Standarduniform für die Waffen-SS war. Er trägt Standard-Marschstiefel bis über die Knie und ein 7,92mm-Gewehr Kar 98k. Am Gürtel de hölzerne Halfter für eine automatische 9mm-Mauserpistole C96. D2 Diese Schittdarstellung der Mauserpistole C96 zeigt das normale 10-schüssige Magazin, von oben her geladen. Ein Schalthebel ermöglichte das Feuern entweder von einzelnen oder von kontinuierlichen Schüssen.

E1 Der normale feldgraue Stahlhelm mit gefaltetem Ranmd und einem sommerlichen Tarnbelag; das SS-Zeichen ersetzte de Armee-Adler auf der rechten Seite. E2 Die Feldmütze mit bogenförmigem Rand ersetzte die frühere Seitenkappe. E3 Ab 1943 wurde die frühere Seitenkappe weithin durch die Einheitsfeldmütze ersetzt; sie beruhte auf der Gebirgsjägerkappe und wurde in verschiedenen Versionen angefertigt; diese mit den zwei Knöpfen war die verbreitetste Art. Der Adler konnte links oder vorne getragen werden – angenäht über dem Totenkopf. E4 Eine leichtgewichtige Version der Feldmütze aus Tarnmaterial. E5 Eine pelzgefütterte Mütze mit langen Ohrenschützern gegen die extreme Kälte des russischen Winters.

F1 Das ist die frühe Siebdruck-Bluse, zuerst getragen bei der Invasion Polens und des Westens. Gezeigt wird hier das Sommermuster, doch ist das Herbstmuster innen im Kragen sichtbar. F2 Eine späte Tarnbluse; die Brusteinschnitte wurden durch aufgesetzte Taschen am unteren Blusenrand ersetzt. Am Hals waren die Zugschnüre durch Knöpfe ersetzt, und die Taille ist höher als bei früheren Versionen. De Bluse hat das Herbstmuster außen, das Sommermuster innen. F3 Die meisten Zeltbahnen waren entweder feldgrau oder in Armee- Tarnmuster, doch gegen Kriegsende erschien gelegentlich das SS-Tarnmuster. F4 Eine Vorderansicht des normalen grau-weißen, reversiblen Winter-Anoraks mit Kapuze, verwendet von der Armee ebenso wie von der SS. Zwecks Wärme war de Anorak mit Deckenmaterial gefüttert und besaß eine Sturmklappe am Hals. F5 Rückenansicht der reversiblen SS-Winterbluse.

G Ein junger Grenadier der 12. SS-Panzerdivision 'Hitlerjugend', dem ein Gefreiter de Bedienung der Panzerfaust erklärt.

H Ein Tankabwehr-Team in den Ardennen während der letzten Offensive im Westen. Sie sind ausgerüstet mit der zweiten Version des Panzerschrecks mit Schild un einem Paar von Anti-Tank-Tellerminen. Der ladende Soldat klopft auf die Schulter des Grenadiers, der den Panzerschreck bedient, um ihm anzuzeigen, daß die Waffe nun geladen ist.

I Dieser Leutnant trägt die Offizierskappe alten Stils, eine Tarnjacke von 1943 und eine Hose von 1944. Er trägt ferner halbhohe Stiefel mit Segeltuchgamaschen anstatt der bis dahin üblichen, übers Knie reichenden Marschstiefel. Rang- und Einheitsabzeichen fehlen, doch wurde ein SS-Adler an den Ärmel genäht. Er ist bewaffnet mit einer 9mm-Erma MPE-Maschenpistole und einer Walther P38 im Halfter. I2 Die 9mm-Walther P38 war seit 1940 die deutsche Standard-Handfeuerwaffe und verfügte über mehrere Konstruktionsverbesserungen gegenüber der Luger, darunter einen besser geformten Griff und Hahn sowie einen Sicherungsstift, der anzeigte, daß sich eine Patrone im Verschluß befand.